I0606027

To:

From:

Date:

The
Everyday
Prayer
MAP®
JOURNAL

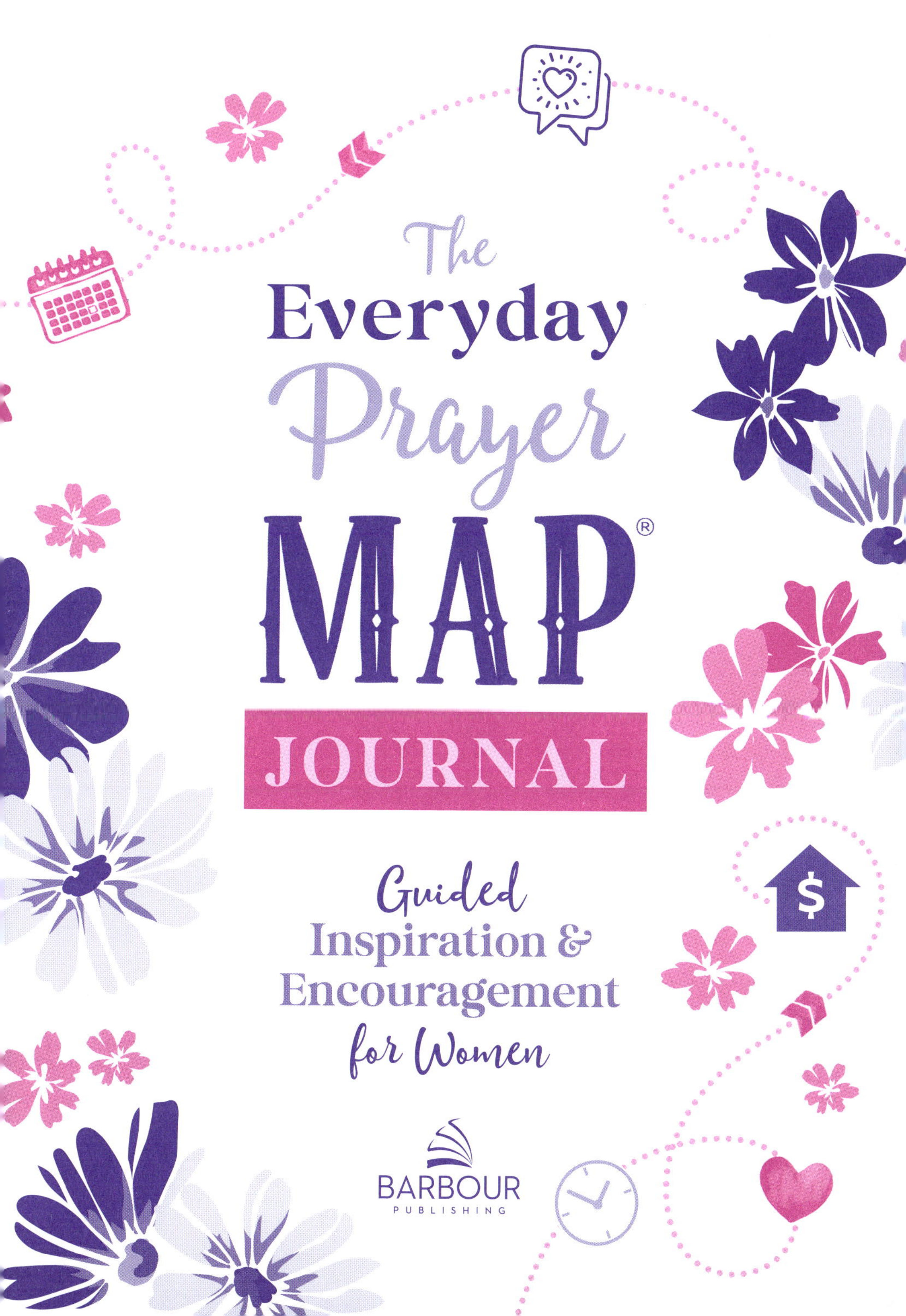
The
Everyday
Prayer
MAP®
JOURNAL
Guided
Inspiration &
Encouragement
for Women
BARBOUR
PUBLISHING

ISBN 979-8-89151-090-6

Published by Barbour Publishing, Inc., 1810 Barbour Drive, Uhrichsville, Ohio 44683, www.barbourbooks.com.

Our mission is to inspire the world with the life-changing message of the Bible.

Printed in China.

INTRODUCTION

Barbour's The Prayer Map journals are perennial bestsellers, with more than half a million copies sold. Now, *The Everyday Prayer Map Journal* provides you with page after page of guided "maps" to follow as you talk to God about things that matter most to your heart. Whether you're experiencing anxiety, grief, fear, stress, hopelessness, hardship, or something more, this journal is overflowing with daily, practical, purposeful prayer maps to help you more fully experience the life-changing power of prayer in your life. Throughout this journal, you'll be prompted to create your very own Prayer Maps (already outlined in a colorful design), resulting in helpful guides for your personal prayer time. You can follow your Prayer Maps—from start to finish!—as you talk to God each day.

Each map includes a spot to record the date, so you can look back on your prayers and see how God has listened, loved, and answered. *The Everyday Prayer Map Journal* will help you build a healthy spiritual habit of continual prayer for life!

Sections Include:

1. When You Just Need to Talk to God (page 9)
2. When You Need a Boost of Courage (page 63)
3. When You're Worried (page 117)
4. When You're Going through a Difficult Time (page 171)
5. When You Don't Know What to Pray (page 223)
6. When You Need Hope and Healing (page 277)
7. When You Want a Good Start to Your Morning (page 329)

Section 1: When You Just Need to Talk to God

BE THE BRIDGE

"I looked for someone among them who would build up the wall and stand before me in the gap on behalf of the land so I would not have to destroy it, but I found no one."
EZEKIEL 22:30 NIV

Each prayer request you offer up to God is important to you, and when you ask others to pray, you're counting on them to help carry you through the tough times.

Do you give the same consideration to those who ask you for prayer? It's easy in the busyness of life to overlook a request someone else has made. Maybe you don't know the person very well or you don't really understand what he or she is going through. Perhaps the request came in a text that you quickly glanced at and then deleted. Yet even with texted prayer requests, others trust you to stand in the gap for them during difficult times in their lives.

Don't delay. Take time right when you receive a request to talk to the Lord on the requester's behalf. Be the bridge that carries that person through the valley of darkness back to the mountaintop of joy.

Heavenly Father, help me to have a heart of compassion for those I know—and even for those I don't know—who need Your comfort and love. Help me never to be too busy to pray for them. Amen.

Date:

Dear Heavenly Father,

Thank You for. . .

People I am praying for today. . .

I am worried about. . .

Here's what's happening in my life. . .

I need. . .

Other things on my heart that I need to share with You, God. . .

Thank You, Father, for hearing my prayers. Amen.

"O Lord, please hear my prayer! Listen to the prayers of those of us who delight in honoring you."
NEHEMIAH 1:11 NLT

Date:

Dear Heavenly Father,

Thank You for...

People I am praying for today...

I am worried about...

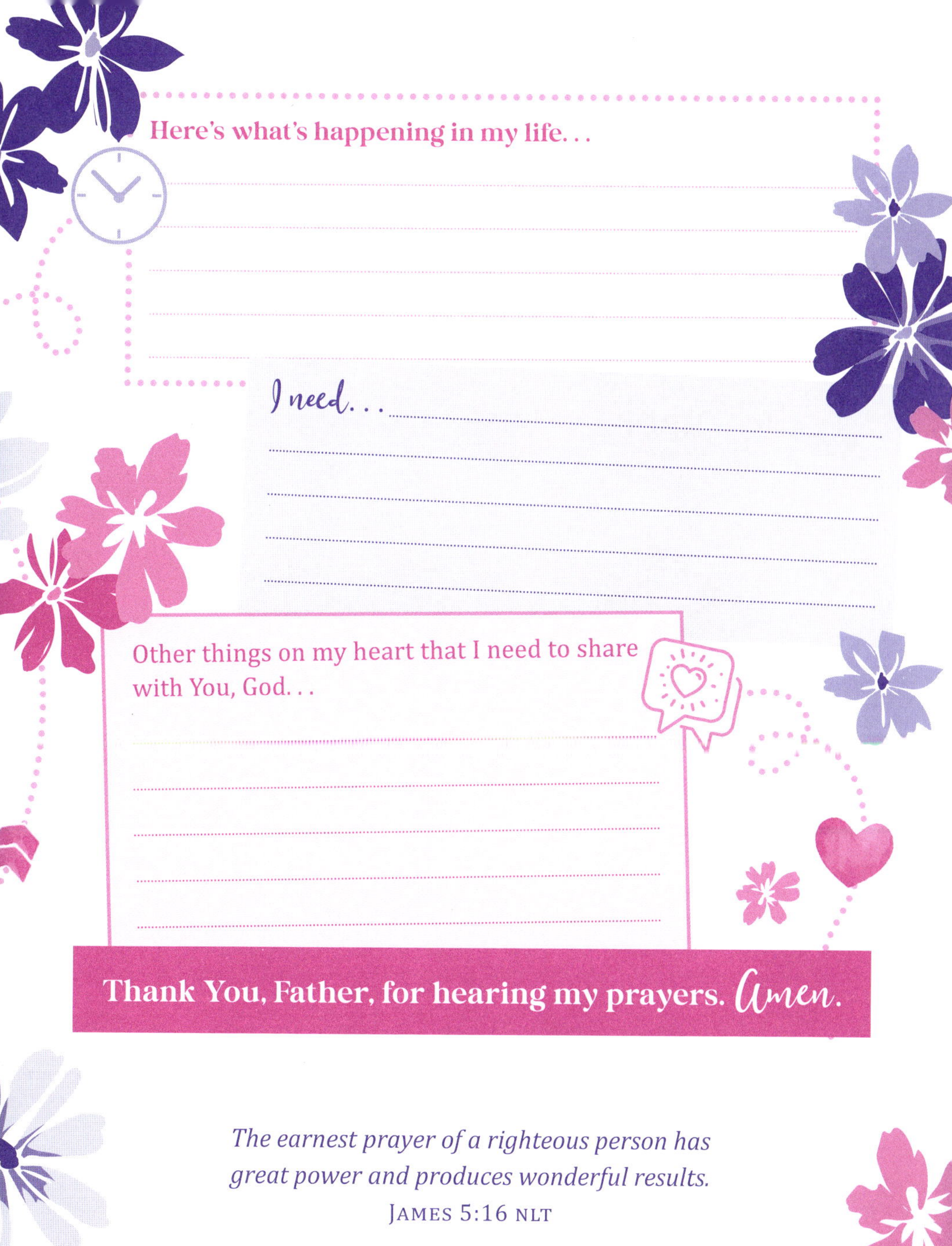

Here's what's happening in my life. . .

I need. . .

Other things on my heart that I need to share with You, God. . .

Thank You, Father, for hearing my prayers. Amen.

The earnest prayer of a righteous person has great power and produces wonderful results.
JAMES 5:16 NLT

Date:

Dear Heavenly Father,

Thank You for...

People I am praying for today...

I am worried about...

Here's what's happening in my life. . .

I need. . .

Other things on my heart that I need to share with You, God. . .

Thank You, Father, for hearing my prayers. *Amen.*

Listen to my cry for help, my King and my God, for I pray to no one but you.

PSALM 5:2 NLT

Date:

Dear Heavenly Father,

Thank You for...

People I am praying for today...

I am worried about...

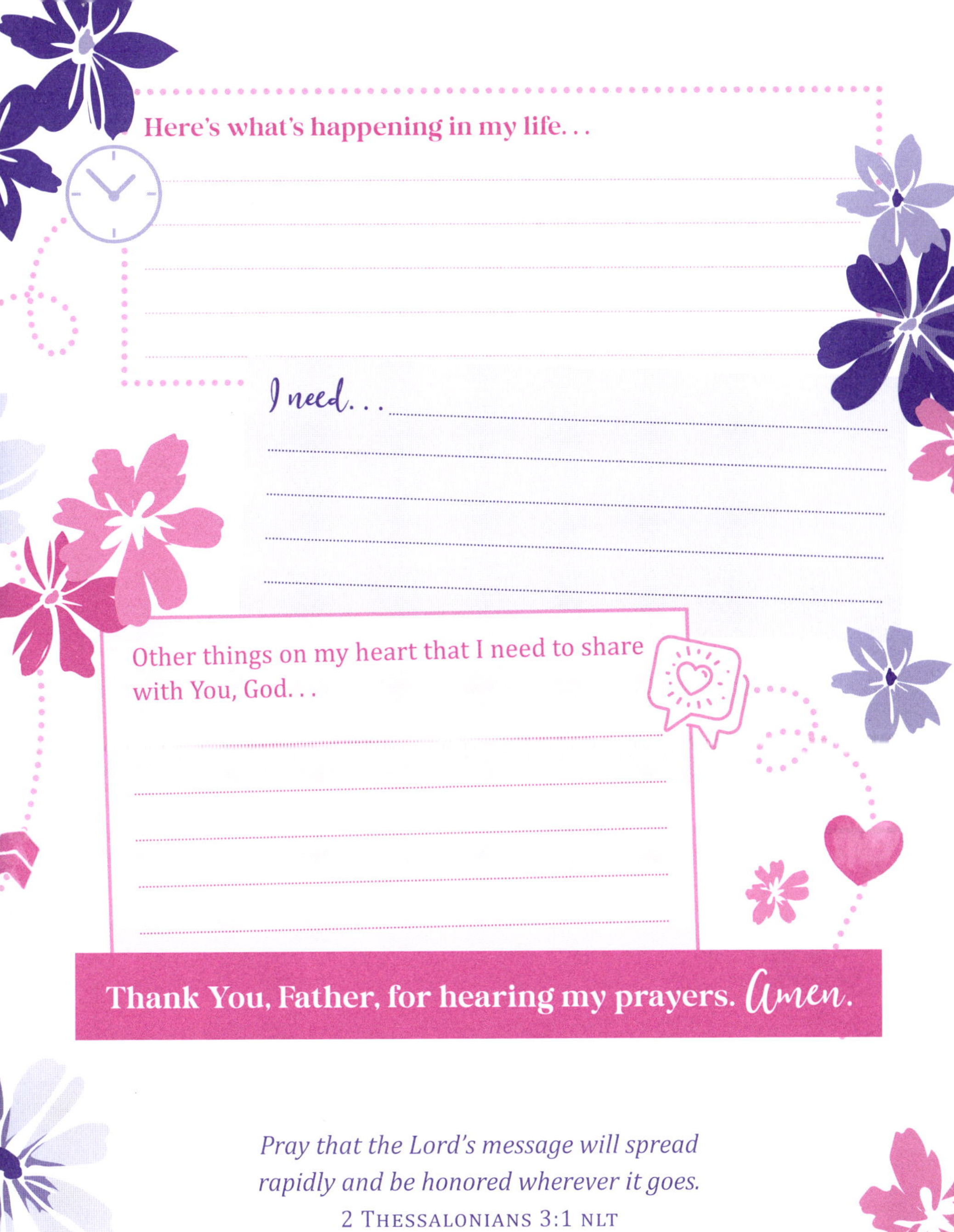

Pray that the Lord's message will spread rapidly and be honored wherever it goes.
2 Thessalonians 3:1 NLT

Date:

Dear Heavenly Father,

Thank You for...

People I am praying for today...

I am worried about...

Here's what's happening in my life. . .

I need. . .

Other things on my heart that I need to share with You, God. . .

Thank You, Father, for hearing my prayers. Amen.

"Keep on asking, and you will receive what you ask for. Keep on seeking, and you will find. Keep on knocking, and the door will be opened to you."
MATTHEW 7:7 NLT

Date:

Dear Heavenly Father,

Thank You for...

People I am praying for today...

I am worried about...

Here's what's happening in my life. . .

I need. . .

Other things on my heart that I need to share with You, God. . .

Thank You, Father, for hearing my prayers. Amen.

Hear me as I pray, O Lord.
Be merciful and answer me!
Psalm 27:7 NLT

Date:

Dear Heavenly Father,

Thank You for...

People I am praying for today...

I am worried about...

Here's what's happening in my life. . .

I need. . .

Other things on my heart that I need to share with You, God. . .

Thank You, Father, for hearing my prayers. *Amen.*

Devote yourselves to prayer with an alert mind and a thankful heart.

Colossians 4:2 NLT

Date:

Dear Heavenly Father,

Thank You for...

People I am praying for today...

I am worried about...

Here's what's happening in my life. . .

I need. . .

Other things on my heart that I need to share with You, God. . .

Thank You, Father, for hearing my prayers. *Amen.*

"O Lord, you are a great and awesome God! You always fulfill your covenant and keep your promises of unfailing love to those who love you and obey your commands."

DANIEL 9:4 NLT

Date:

Dear Heavenly Father,

Thank You for. . .

People I am praying for today. . .

I am worried about. . .

Here's what's happening in my life. . .

I need. . .

Other things on my heart that I need to share with You, God. . .

Thank You, Father, for hearing my prayers. *Amen.*

But each day the L*ORD pours his unfailing love upon me, and through each night I sing his songs, praying to God who gives me life.*

PSALM 42:8 NLT

Date:

Dear Heavenly Father,

Thank You for. . .

People I am praying for today. . .

I am worried about. . .

Here's what's happening in my life. . .

I need. . .

Other things on my heart that I need to share with You, God. . .

Thank You, Father, for hearing my prayers. *Amen.*

I pray that God, the source of hope, will fill you completely with joy and peace because you trust in him.

ROMANS 15:13 NLT

Date:

Dear Heavenly Father,

Thank You for. . .

People I am praying for today. . .

I am worried about. . .

Here's what's happening in my life. . .

I need. . .

Other things on my heart that I need to share with You, God. . .

Thank You, Father, for hearing my prayers. Amen.

"Pray with all your might!
And don't let up!"
1 Samuel 7:8 msg

Date:

Dear Heavenly Father,

Thank You for. . .

People I am praying for today. . .

I am worried about. . .

We always pray for you, and we give thanks to God, the Father of our Lord Jesus Christ.

COLOSSIANS 1:3 NLT

Date:

Dear Heavenly Father,

Thank You for. . .

People I am praying for today. . .

I am worried about. . .

Here's what's happening in my life. . .

I need. . .

Other things on my heart that I need to share with You, God. . .

Thank You, Father, for hearing my prayers. *Amen*.

Pray for all people. Ask God to help them; intercede on their behalf, and give thanks for them.

1 Timothy 2:1 NLT

Date:

Dear Heavenly Father,

Thank You for. . .

People I am praying for today. . .

I am worried about. . .

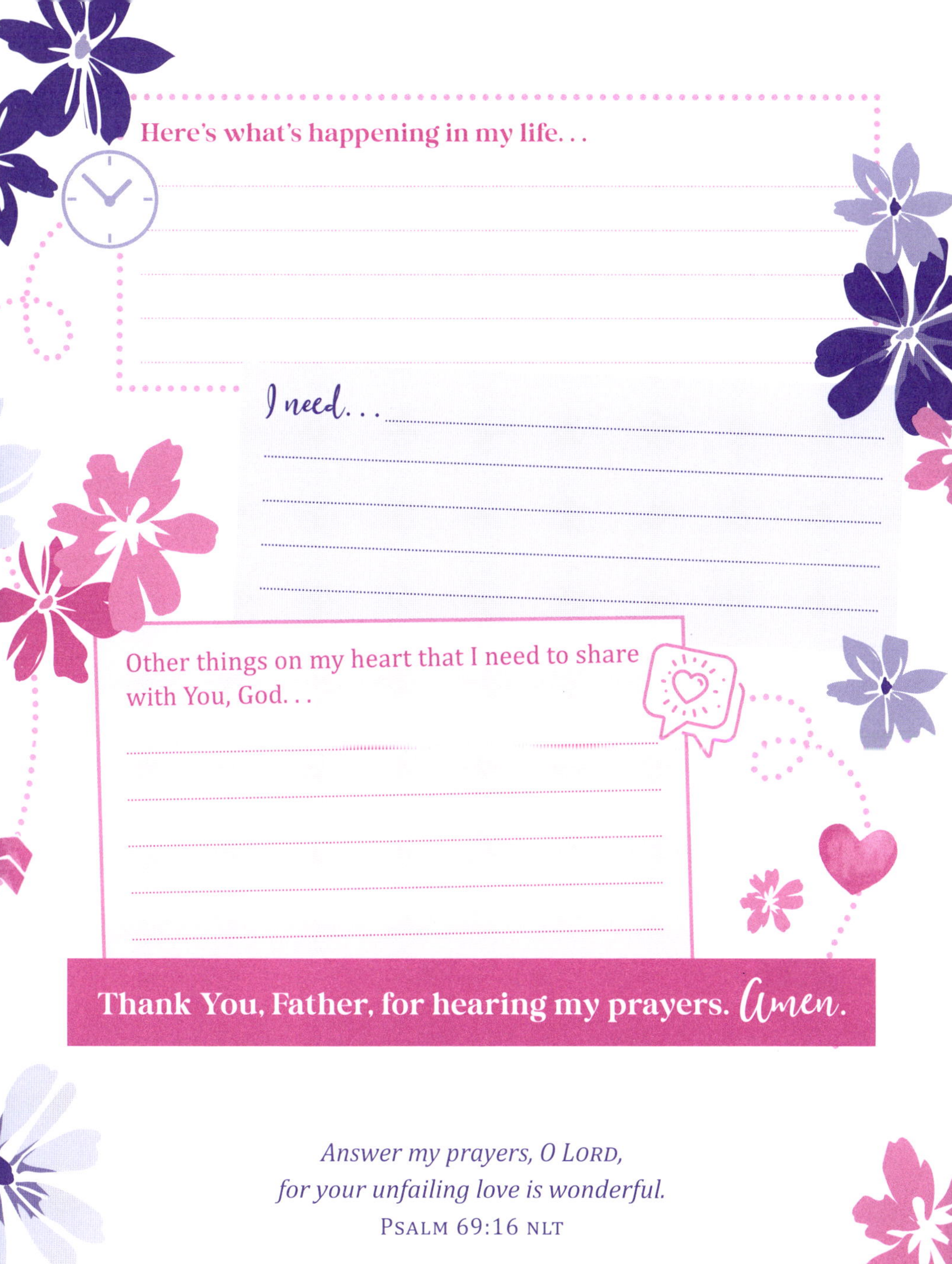

Answer my prayers, O Lord,
for your unfailing love is wonderful.
Psalm 69:16 NLT

Date:

Dear Heavenly Father,

Thank You for. . .

People I am praying for today. . .

I am worried about. . .

They will pray for you with deep affection because of the overflowing grace God has given to you.
2 Corinthians 9:14 NLT

Date:

Dear Heavenly Father,

Thank You for. . .

People I am praying for today. . .

I am worried about. . .

Here's what's happening in my life. . .

I need. . .

Other things on my heart that I need to share with You, God. . .

Thank You, Father, for hearing my prayers. Amen.

Because he bends down to listen,
I will pray as long as I have breath!
PSALM 116:2 NLT

Date:

Dear Heavenly Father,

Thank You for...

People I am praying for today...

I am worried about...

Here's what's happening in my life. . .

I need. . .

Other things on my heart that I need to share with You, God. . .

Thank You, Father, for hearing my prayers. Amen.

I pray that from his glorious, unlimited resources he will empower you with inner strength through his Spirit.
EPHESIANS 3:16 NLT

Date:

Dear Heavenly Father,

Thank You for...

People I am praying for today...

I am worried about...

Here's what's happening in my life. . .

I need. . .

Other things on my heart that I need to share with You, God. . .

Thank You, Father, for hearing my prayers. Amen.

God's way of putting people right shows up in the acts of faith, confirming what Scripture has said all along: "The person in right standing before God by trusting him really lives."

ROMANS 1:17 MSG

Date:

Dear Heavenly Father,

Thank You for. . .

People I am praying for today. . .

I am worried about. . .

Here's what's happening in my life. . .

I need. . .

Other things on my heart that I need to share with You, God. . .

Thank You, Father, for hearing my prayers. Amen.

I lift my hands to you in prayer. I thirst for you as parched land thirsts for rain.

Psalm 143:6 NLT

Date:

Dear Heavenly Father,

Thank You for. . .

People I am praying for today. . .

I am worried about. . .

Here's what's happening in my life. . .

I need. . .

Other things on my heart that I need to share with You, God. . .

Thank You, Father, for hearing my prayers. *Amen.*

"Bless those who curse you. Pray for those who hurt you."
LUKE 6:28 NLT

Date:

Dear Heavenly Father,

Thank You for...

People I am praying for today...

I am worried about...

Here's what's happening in my life...

I need...

Other things on my heart that I need to share with You, God...

Thank You, Father, for hearing my prayers. Amen.

I pray that your love will overflow more and more, and that you will keep on growing in knowledge and understanding.
PHILIPPIANS 1:9 NLT

Date:

Dear Heavenly Father,

Thank You for. . .

People I am praying for today. . .

I am worried about. . .

Here's what's happening in my life. . .

I need. . .

Other things on my heart that I need to share with You, God. . .

Thank You, Father, for hearing my prayers. *Amen.*

"Love your enemies! Pray for those who persecute you!"
Matthew 5:44 NLT

Date:

Dear Heavenly Father,

Thank You for. . .

People I am praying for today. . .

I am worried about. . .

Here's what's happening in my life. . .

I need. . .

Other things on my heart that I need to share with You, God. . .

Thank You, Father, for hearing my prayers. *Amen.*

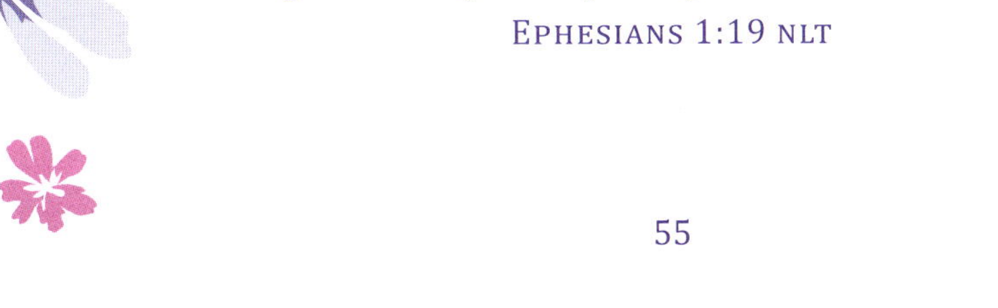

I also pray that you will understand the incredible greatness of God's power for us who believe him.

EPHESIANS 1:19 NLT

Date:

Dear Heavenly Father,

Thank You for...

People I am praying for today...

I am worried about...

Here's what's happening in my life. . .

I need. . .

Other things on my heart that I need to share with You, God. . .

Thank You, Father, for hearing my prayers. *Amen.*

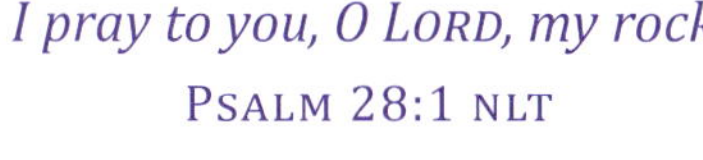

I pray to you, O Lord, my rock.

Psalm 28:1 NLT

Date:

Dear Heavenly Father,

Thank You for. . .

People I am praying for today. . .

I am worried about. . .

Here's what's happening in my life. . .

I need. . .

Other things on my heart that I need to share with You, God. . .

Thank You, Father, for hearing my prayers. Amen.

"You can pray for anything, and if you have faith, you will receive it."
MATTHEW 21:22 NLT

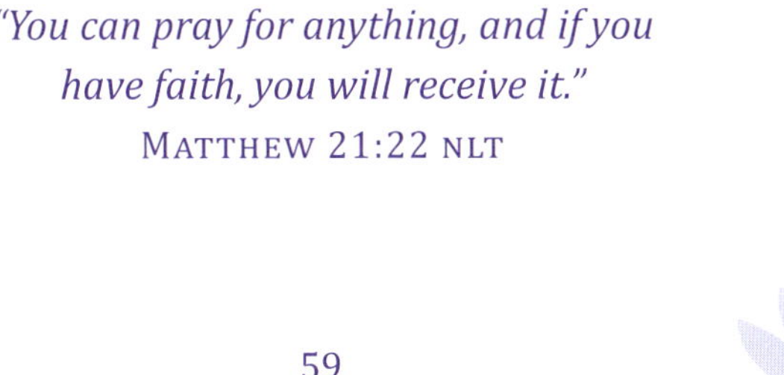

Date:

Dear Heavenly Father,

Thank You for. . .

People I am praying for today. . .

I am worried about. . .

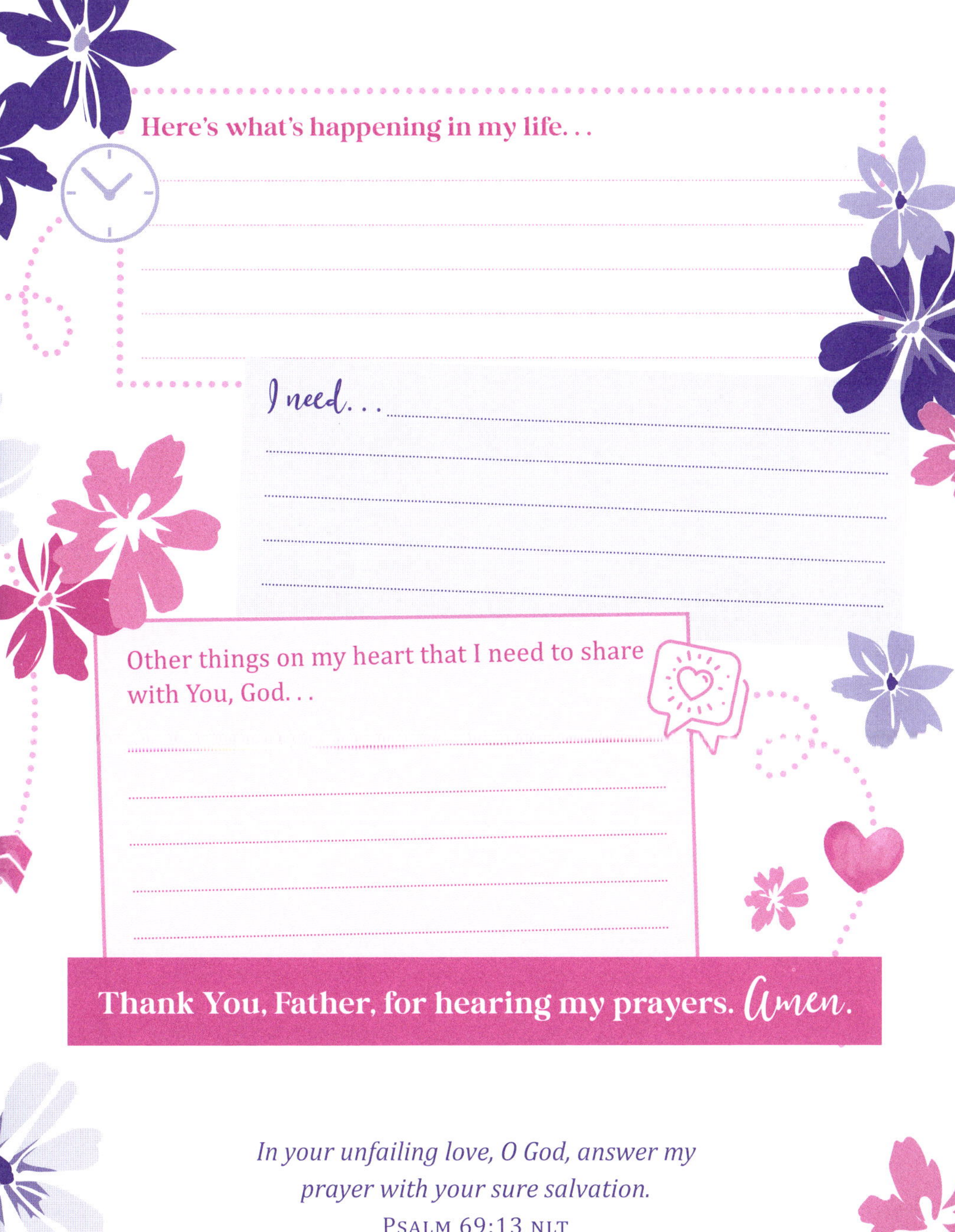

In your unfailing love, O God, answer my prayer with your sure salvation.

PSALM 69:13 NLT

Section 2: When You Need a Boost of Courage

A STRONG HEART

Whom have I in heaven but you? And earth has nothing I desire besides you. My flesh and my heart may fail, but God is the strength of my heart and my portion forever.

PSALM 73:25–26 NIV

Do you ever feel like you have a weak heart? Feel like you're not strong? You crater at every little thing? Do you face life's challenges with your emotions in turmoil instead of facing them head-on with courage and strength? If so, you're not alone. Twenty-first-century women are told they can "be it all" and "do it all," but it's not true. God never meant for us to be strong every moment of our lives. If we were, we wouldn't need Him.

Here's the good news: You don't have to be strong. In your weakness, God's strength shines through. And His strength surpasses anything you could produce, even on your best day. It's the same strength that spoke the heavens and the earth into existence. The same strength that parted the Red Sea. And it's the same strength that made the journey up the hill to the cross.

So how do you tap into that strength? There's only one way. Come into His presence. Spend some quiet time with Him. Acknowledge your weakness, then allow His strong arms to encompass you. There's really nothing else in heaven or on earth to compare. God is all you will ever need.

Father, I feel so weak at times. It's hard just to put one foot in front of the other. But I know You are my strength. Invigorate me with that strength today, Lord.

Date:

Dear Heavenly Father,

My gutsy prayer for today is. . .

I need You to. . .

With You by my side, I am unafraid because. . .

I believe You are the doer of the impossible because. . .

I know You will. . .

Please give me the strength and courage I need today.

Thank You, Father, for hearing my prayers. Amen.

Light, space, zest—that's God! So, with him on my side I'm fearless, afraid of no one and nothing.

Psalm 27:1 msg

Date:

Dear Heavenly Father,

My gutsy prayer for today is. . .

I need You to. . .

With You by my side, I am unafraid because. . .

I have the strength to face all conditions
by the power that Christ gives me.
PHILIPPIANS 4:13 GNT

Date:

Dear Heavenly Father,

My gutsy prayer for today is. . .

I need You to. . .

With You by my side, I am unafraid because. . .

I believe You are the doer of the impossible because. . .

I know You will. . .

Please give me the strength and courage I need today.

Thank You, Father, for hearing my prayers. *Amen.*

"Don't panic. I'm with you. There's no need to fear for I'm your God. I'll give you strength. I'll help you. I'll hold you steady, keep a firm grip on you."

Isaiah 41:10 msg

Date:

Dear Heavenly Father,

My gutsy prayer for today is. . .

I need You to. . .

With You by my side, I am unafraid because. . .

I believe You are the doer of the impossible because. . .

I know You will. . .

Please give me the strength and courage I need today.

Thank You, Father, for hearing my prayers. Amen.

The Lord is my strong defender; he is the one who has saved me. He is my God, and I will praise him, my father's God, and I will sing about his greatness.

Exodus 15:2 GNT

Date:

Dear Heavenly Father,

My gutsy prayer for today is. . .

I need You to. . .

With You by my side, I am unafraid because. . .

I believe You are the doer of the impossible because. . .

I know You will. . .

Please give me the strength and courage I need today.

Thank You, Father, for hearing my prayers. Amen.

Don't you know? Haven't you heard? The eternal God, the Lord, the Creator of the ends of the earth, doesn't grow tired or become weary. His understanding is beyond reach.

Isaiah 40:28–29 gw

Date:

Dear Heavenly Father,

My gutsy prayer for today is. . .

I need You to. . .

With You by my side, I am unafraid because. . .

I believe You are the doer of the impossible because. . .

I know You will. . .

Please give me the strength and courage I need today.

Thank You, Father, for hearing my prayers. *Amen.*

The Scriptures impart to us encouragement and inspiration so that we can live in hope and endure all things.

Romans 15:4 TPT

Date:

Dear Heavenly Father,

My gutsy prayer for today is. . .

I need You to. . .

With You by my side, I am unafraid because. . .

I believe You are the doer of the impossible because. . .

I know You will. . .

Please give me the strength and courage I need today.

Thank You, Father, for hearing my prayers. Amen.

God is my savior; I will trust him and not be afraid.
The LORD gives me power and strength; he is my savior.
ISAIAH 12:2 GNT

Date:

Dear Heavenly Father,

My gutsy prayer for today is. . .

I need You to. . .

With You by my side, I am unafraid because. . .

I believe You are the doer of the impossible because...

I know You will...

Please give me the strength and courage I need today.

Thank You, Father, for hearing my prayers. Amen.

Lord, so many times I fail; I fall into disgrace. But when I trust in you, I have a strong and glorious presence protecting and anointing me. Forever you're all I need!

PSALM 73:26 TPT

Date:

Dear Heavenly Father,

My gutsy prayer for today is. . .

I need You to. . .

With You by my side, I am unafraid because. . .

I believe You are the doer of the impossible because. . .

I know You will. . .

Please give me the strength and courage I need today.

Thank You, Father, for hearing my prayers. *Amen.*

The LORD is my light and my salvation; I will fear no one.
The LORD protects me from all danger; I will never be afraid.
PSALM 27:1 GNT

Date:

Dear Heavenly Father,

My gutsy prayer for today is. . .

I need You to. . .

With You by my side, I am unafraid because. . .

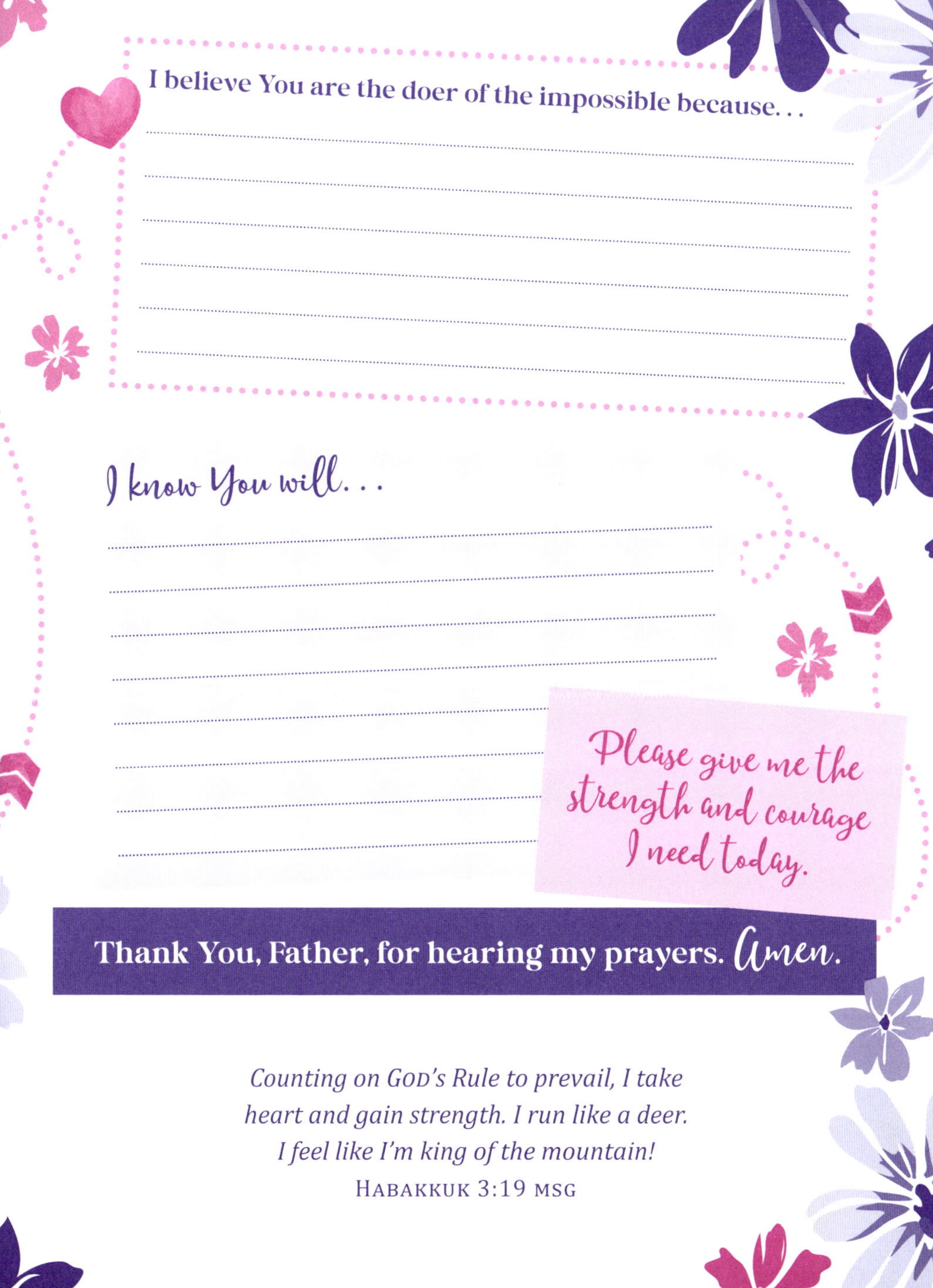

I believe You are the doer of the impossible because. . .

I know You will. . .

Please give me the strength and courage I need today.

Thank You, Father, for hearing my prayers. Amen.

Counting on God's Rule to prevail, I take
heart and gain strength. I run like a deer.
I feel like I'm king of the mountain!
Habakkuk 3:19 msg

Date:

Dear Heavenly Father,

My gutsy prayer for today is. . .

I need You to. . .

With You by my side, I am unafraid because. . .

I believe You are the doer of the impossible because. . .

I know You will. . .

Please give me the strength and courage I need today.

Thank You, Father, for hearing my prayers. *Amen.*

"In this godless world you will continue to experience difficulties. But take heart! I've conquered the world."
JOHN 16:33 MSG

Date:

Dear Heavenly Father,

My gutsy prayer for today is. . .

I need You to. . .

With You by my side, I am unafraid because. . .

I believe You are the doder of the impossible because. . .

I know You will. . .

Please give me the strength and courage I need today.

Thank You, Father, for hearing my prayers. Amen.

Jesus. . .addressed them: "I am the world's Light. No one who follows me stumbles around in the darkness. I provide plenty of light to live in."
John 8:12 MSG

Date:

Dear Heavenly Father,

My gutsy prayer for today is. . .

I need You to. . .

With You by my side, I am unafraid because. . .

I believe You are the doer of the impossible because. . .

I know You will. . .

Please give me the strength and courage I need today.

Thank You, Father, for hearing my prayers. Amen.

They pushed hard to make me fall, but the LORD helped me.
The LORD is my strength and my song. He is my savior.
PSALM 118:13–14 GW

Date:

Dear Heavenly Father,

My gutsy prayer for today is...

I need You to...

With You by my side, I am unafraid because...

I believe You are the doer of the impossible because. . .

I know You will. . .

Please give me the strength and courage I need today.

Thank You, Father, for hearing my prayers. Amen.

The Lord protects and defends me; I trust in him. He gives me help and makes me glad; I praise him with joyful songs.
Psalm 28:7 GNT

Date:

Dear Heavenly Father,

My gutsy prayer for today is...

I need You to...

With You by my side, I am unafraid because...

I believe You are the doer of the impossible because. . .

I know You will. . .

Please give me the strength and courage I need today.

Thank You, Father, for hearing my prayers. Amen.

I'm asking God to give you a gift from the wealth of his glory. I pray that he would give you inner strength and power through his Spirit.
EPHESIANS 3:16 GW

Date:

Dear Heavenly Father,

My gutsy prayer for today is. . .

I need You to. . .

With You by my side, I am unafraid because. . .

I believe You are the doer of the impossible because. . .

I know You will. . .

Please give me the strength and courage I need today.

Thank You, Father, for hearing my prayers. Amen.

The Lord your God is with you. He is a hero who saves you. He happily rejoices over you, renews you with his love, and celebrates over you with shouts of joy.

Zephaniah 3:17 gw

Date:

Dear Heavenly Father,

My gutsy prayer for today is. . .

I need You to. . .

With You by my side, I am unafraid because. . .

I believe You are the doer of the impossible because. . .

I know You will. . .

Please give me the strength and courage I need today.

Thank You, Father, for hearing my prayers. Amen.

I'm sure now I'll see God's goodness in the exuberant earth. Stay with God! Take heart. Don't quit. I'll say it again: Stay with God.
Psalm 27:13–14 msg

Date:

Dear Heavenly Father,

My gutsy prayer for today is. . .

I need You to. . .

With You by my side, I am unafraid because. . .

I believe You are the doer of the impossible because. . .

I know You will. . .

Please give me the strength and courage I need today.

Thank You, Father, for hearing my prayers. *Amen.*

Thank you for your love, thank you for your faithfulness; most holy is your name, most holy is your Word. The moment I called out, you stepped in; you made my life large with strength.

Psalm 138:2–3 msg

Date:

Dear Heavenly Father,

My gutsy prayer for today is. . .

I need You to. . .

With You by my side, I am unafraid because. . .

I believe You are the doer of the impossible because. . .

I know You will. . .

Please give me the strength and courage I need today.

Thank You, Father, for hearing my prayers. Amen.

God means what he says. What he says goes. . . .
Nothing and no one can resist God's Word.
We can't get away from it—no matter what.
Hebrews 4:12–13 MSG

Date:

Dear Heavenly Father,

My gutsy prayer for today is. . .

I need You to. . .

With You by my side, I am unafraid because. . .

I believe You are the doer of the impossible because. . .

I know You will. . .

Please give me the strength and courage I need today.

Thank You, Father, for hearing my prayers. Amen.

He is the God who makes me strong, who makes my pathway safe. He makes me sure-footed as a deer; he keeps me safe on the mountains. He trains me for battle, so that I can use the strongest bow.

PSALM 18:32–34 GNT

Date:

Dear Heavenly Father,

My gutsy prayer for today is. . .

I need You to. . .

With You by my side, I am unafraid because. . .

I believe You are the doer of the impossible because. . .

I know You will. . .

Please give me the strength and courage I need today.

Thank You, Father, for hearing my prayers. *Amen.*

So be content with who you are, and don't put on airs. God's strong hand is on you; he'll promote you at the right time. Live carefree before God; he is most careful with you.
1 Peter 5:6–7 msg

Date:

Dear Heavenly Father,

My gutsy prayer for today is. . .

I need You to. . .

With You by my side, I am unafraid because. . .

I believe You are the doer of the impossible because. . .

I know You will. . .

Please give me the strength and courage I need today.

Thank You, Father, for hearing my prayers. *Amen.*

"Don't be afraid. You are highly respected. Everything is alright! Be strong! Be strong!"
DANIEL 10:19 GW

Date:

Dear Heavenly Father,

My gutsy prayer for today is. . .

I need You to. . .

With You by my side, I am unafraid because. . .

I believe You are the doer of the impossible because. . .

I know You will. . .

Please give me the strength and courage I need today.

Thank You, Father, for hearing my prayers. Amen.

People cannot save themselves.
But with God, all things are possible.
Matthew 19:26 voice

Date:

Dear Heavenly Father,

My gutsy prayer for today is...

I need You to...

With You by my side, I am unafraid because...

I believe You are the doer of the impossible because. . .

I know You will. . .

Please give me the strength and courage I need today.

Thank You, Father, for hearing my prayers. Amen.

Never doubt God's mighty power. . . . He will achieve infinitely more than your greatest request, your most unbelievable dream, and exceed your wildest imagination!
Ephesians 3:20 TPT

Date:

Dear Heavenly Father,

My gutsy prayer for today is. . .

I need You to. . .

With You by my side, I am unafraid because. . .

I believe You are the doer of the impossible because. . .

I know You will. . .

Please give me the strength and courage I need today.

Thank You, Father, for hearing my prayers. *Amen.*

"Eternal Lord, with Your outstretched arm and Your enormous power You created the heavens and the earth. Nothing is too difficult for You."
JEREMIAH 32:17 VOICE

Date:

Dear Heavenly Father,

My gutsy prayer for today is. . .

I need You to. . .

With You by my side, I am unafraid because. . .

I believe You are the doer of the impossible because. . .

I know You will. . .

Please give me the strength and courage I need today.

Thank You, Father, for hearing my prayers. Amen.

We can't round up enough containers to hold everything God generously pours into our lives through the Holy Spirit!

Romans 5:5 msg

Section 3: When You're Worried

TROUBLE OR TRUST?

"Don't let your hearts be troubled. Trust in God, and trust also in me."
John 14:1 NLT

Trouble or trust? Which will you choose today? We women tend to be troubled in our hearts, worrying about our relationships, our appearance, our finances, our work, and perhaps especially about the future.

The disciples were worried about their future as well. Jesus had told them He would be going away from them. He was preparing them for His death, resurrection, and ascension into heaven. They were saddened when they heard Him say that they could not come with Him at that time, although they would follow later.

So Christ spoke these words to them in John 14:1, reminding them to trust in God and to trust in Him. He told them not to let their hearts be troubled. Sometimes we feel as if we can't control feeling troubled. But when we focus on the Lord and meditate upon His promises, we can gain control of our worries and replace them with trust.

You do not know what your future holds, but God does. He asks you to stop worrying. He asks you to trust in Him. He is faithful to provide for His own.

Father, please replace trouble with trust in this heart of mine that is sometimes lonely and unsure of the future. Thank You, Lord, that I can trust in You. Amen.

Date:

Dear Heavenly Father,

Nothing is too hard for You. You can—*and will*—handle everything that comes my way, including. . .

Here's what's happening in my life right now. . .

And here's where I need Your reassuring presence, Father. . .

When worries threaten to overwhelm me, please help me to fix my mind on things that truly deserve my focus, like. . .

I trust You to. . .

I leave everything in Your mighty hands, God.

Thank You, Father, for hearing my prayers. Amen.

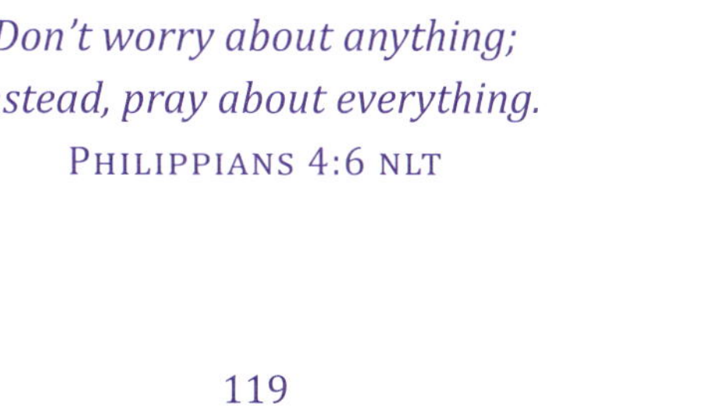

Don't worry about anything;
instead, pray about everything.
PHILIPPIANS 4:6 NLT

Date:

Dear Heavenly Father,

Nothing is too hard for You. You can—*and will*—handle everything that comes my way, including. . .

Here's what's happening in my life right now. . .

And here's where I need Your reassuring presence, Father. . .

When worries threaten to overwhelm me, please help me to fix my mind on things that truly deserve my focus, like. . .

I trust You to. . .

I leave everything in Your mighty hands, God.

Thank You, Father, for hearing my prayers. *Amen.*

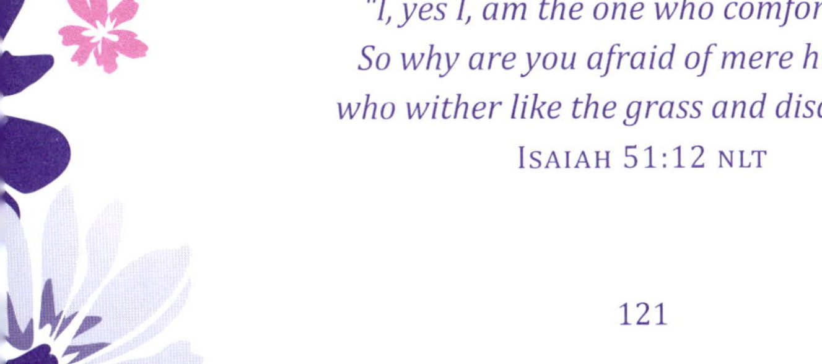

"I, yes I, am the one who comforts you.
So why are you afraid of mere humans,
who wither like the grass and disappear?"
Isaiah 51:12 NLT

Date:

Dear Heavenly Father,

Nothing is too hard for You. You can—*and will*—handle everything that comes my way, including. . .

Here's what's happening in my life right now. . .

And here's where I need Your reassuring presence, Father. . .

When worries threaten to overwhelm me, please help me to fix my mind on things that truly deserve my focus, like. . .

I trust You to. . .

I leave everything in Your mighty hands, God.

Thank You, Father, for hearing my prayers. Amen.

You have done many miraculous things,
O LORD my God. You have made many wonderful
plans for us. No one compares to you!
PSALM 40:5 GW

Date:

Dear Heavenly Father,

Nothing is too hard for You. You can—*and will*—handle everything that comes my way, including. . .

Here's what's happening in my life right now. . .

And here's where I need Your reassuring presence, Father. . .

When worries threaten to overwhelm me, please help me to fix my mind on things that truly deserve my focus, like. . .

I trust You to. . .

I leave everything in Your mighty hands, God.

Thank You, Father, for hearing my prayers. *Amen.*

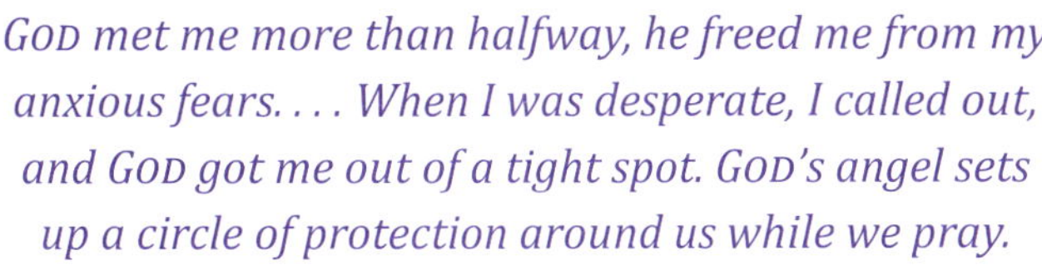

God met me more than halfway, he freed me from my anxious fears. . . . When I was desperate, I called out, and God got me out of a tight spot. God's angel sets up a circle of protection around us while we pray.

Psalm 34:4, 6–7 msg

Date:

Dear Heavenly Father,

Nothing is too hard for You. You can—*and will*—handle everything that comes my way, including. . .

Here's what's happening in my life right now. . .

And here's where I need Your reassuring presence, Father. . .

When worries threaten to overwhelm me, please help me to fix my mind on things that truly deserve my focus, like. . .

I trust You to. . .

I leave everything in Your mighty hands, God.

Thank You, Father, for hearing my prayers. Amen.

I love the L*ORD because he hears my voice and my prayer for mercy. Because he bends down to listen, I will pray as long as I have breath!*

PSALM 116:1–2 NLT

Date:

Dear Heavenly Father,

Nothing is too hard for You. You can—*and will*—handle everything that comes my way, including. . .

Here's what's happening in my life right now. . .

And here's where I need Your reassuring presence, Father. . .

When worries threaten to overwhelm me, please help me to fix my mind on things that truly deserve my focus, like. . .

I trust You to. . .

I leave everything in Your mighty hands, God.

Thank You, Father, for hearing my prayers. Amen.

The LORD will give power to his people.
The LORD will bless his people with peace.
PSALM 29:11 GW

Date:

Dear Heavenly Father,

Nothing is too hard for You. You can—*and will*—handle everything that comes my way, including. . .

Here's what's happening in my life right now. . .

And here's where I need Your reassuring presence, Father. . .

When worries threaten to overwhelm me, please help me to fix my mind on things that truly deserve my focus, like. . .

I trust You to. . .

I leave everything in Your mighty hands, God.

Thank You, Father, for hearing my prayers. Amen.

I know and rest in confidence upon it that the Lord will maintain the cause of the afflicted, and will secure justice for the poor and needy.

Psalm 140:12 AMPC

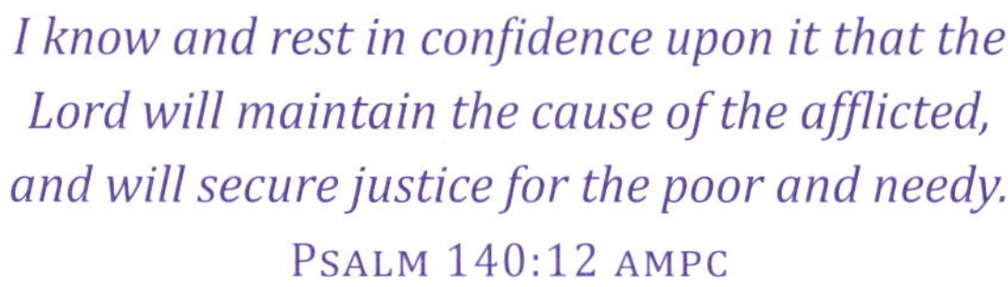

Date:

Dear Heavenly Father,

Nothing is too hard for You. You can—*and will*—handle everything that comes my way, including. . .

Here's what's happening in my life right now. . .

And here's where I need Your reassuring presence, Father. . .

When worries threaten to overwhelm me, please help me to fix my mind on things that truly deserve my focus, like. . .

I trust You to. . .

I leave everything in Your mighty hands, God.

Thank You, Father, for hearing my prayers. *Amen.*

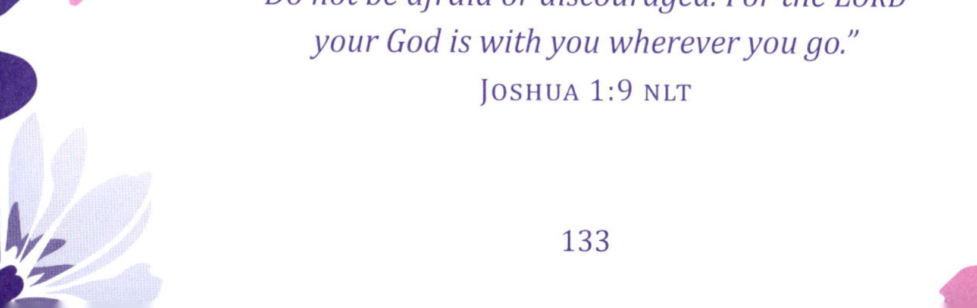

"This is my command—be strong and courageous! Do not be afraid or discouraged. For the LORD your God is with you wherever you go."

JOSHUA 1:9 NLT

Date:
Dear Heavenly Father,
Nothing is too hard for You. You can—*and will*—handle everything that comes my way, including. . .
Here's what's happening in my life right now. . .
And here's where I need Your reassuring presence, Father. . .

When worries threaten to overwhelm me, please help me to fix my mind on things that truly deserve my focus, like. . .

I trust You to. . .

I leave everything in Your mighty hands, God.

Thank You, Father, for hearing my prayers. *Amen.*

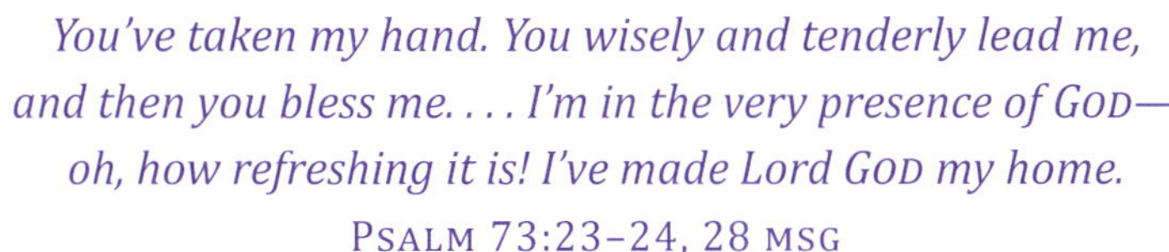

You've taken my hand. You wisely and tenderly lead me, and then you bless me. . . . I'm in the very presence of God— oh, how refreshing it is! I've made Lord God my home.

Psalm 73:23–24, 28 msg

Date:

Dear Heavenly Father,

Nothing is too hard for You. You can—*and will*—handle everything that comes my way, including. . .

Here's what's happening in my life right now. . .

And here's where I need Your reassuring presence, Father. . .

Thank You, Father, for hearing my prayers. *Amen.*

I meditate on all Your doings; I ponder the work of Your hands. . . . Cause me to hear Your loving-kindness in the morning, for on You do I lean and in You do I trust. Cause me to know the way wherein I should walk, for I lift up my inner self to You.

Psalm 143:5, 8 ampc

Date:

Dear Heavenly Father,

Nothing is too hard for You. You can—*and will*—handle everything that comes my way, including. . .

Here's what's happening in my life right now. . .

And here's where I need Your reassuring presence, Father. . .

When worries threaten to overwhelm me, please help me to fix my mind on things that truly deserve my focus, like. . .

I trust You to. . .

I leave everything in Your mighty hands, God.

Thank You, Father, for hearing my prayers. Amen.

Blessed be the Lord, my Rock and my keen and firm Strength. . .my Steadfast Love and my Fortress, my High Tower and my Deliverer, my Shield and He in Whom I trust and take refuge.

Psalm 144:1–2 AMPC

Date:

Dear Heavenly Father,

Nothing is too hard for You. You can—*and will*—handle everything that comes my way, including. . .

Here's what's happening in my life right now. . .

And here's where I need Your reassuring presence, Father. . .

When worries threaten to overwhelm me, please help me to fix my mind on things that truly deserve my focus, like. . .

I trust You to. . .

I leave everything in Your mighty hands, God.

Thank You, Father, for hearing my prayers. *Amen.*

"I will trust, and will not be afraid; for the Lord God is my strength and my song, and he has become my salvation."
Isaiah 12:2 esv

Date:

Dear Heavenly Father,

Nothing is too hard for You. You can—*and will*—handle everything that comes my way, including. . .

Here's what's happening in my life right now. . .

And here's where I need Your reassuring presence, Father. . .

When worries threaten to overwhelm me, please help me to fix my mind on things that truly deserve my focus, like. . .

I trust You to. . .

I leave everything in Your mighty hands, God.

Thank You, Father, for hearing my prayers. *Amen.*

Be earnest and unwearied and steadfast in your prayer [life], being [both] alert and intent in [your praying] with thanksgiving.

COLOSSIANS 4:2 AMPC

Date:

Dear Heavenly Father,

Nothing is too hard for You. You can—*and will*—handle everything that comes my way, including. . .

Here's what's happening in my life right now. . .

And here's where I need Your reassuring presence, Father. . .

When worries threaten to overwhelm me, please help me to fix my mind on things that truly deserve my focus, like. . .

I trust You to. . .

I leave everything in Your mighty hands, God.

Thank You, Father, for hearing my prayers. Amen.

Desperate, I throw myself on you: you are my God! Hour by hour I place my days in your hand. . . . What a stack of blessing you have piled up for those who worship you, ready and waiting for all who run to you to escape an unkind world.

Psalm 31:14–15, 19 msg

Date:

Dear Heavenly Father,

Nothing is too hard for You. You can—*and will*—handle everything that comes my way, including. . .

Here's what's happening in my life right now. . .

And here's where I need Your reassuring presence, Father. . .

When worries threaten to overwhelm me, please help me to fix my mind on things that truly deserve my focus, like. . .

I trust You to. . .

I leave everything in Your mighty hands, God.

Thank You, Father, for hearing my prayers. *Amen.*

God showed how much he loved us by sending his one and only Son into the world so that we might have eternal life through him. This is real love—not that we loved God, but that he loved us.

1 JOHN 4:9–10 NLT

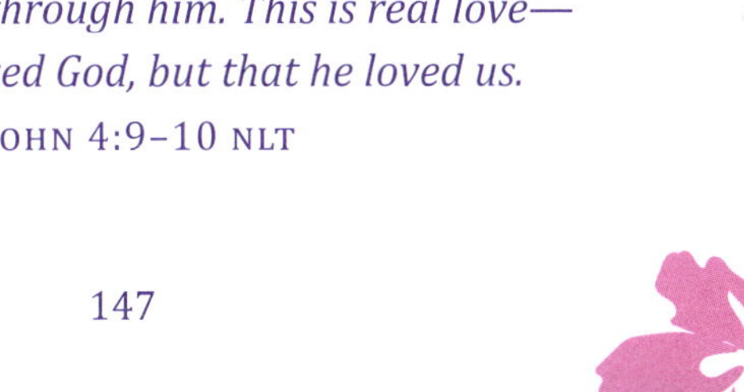

Date:

Dear Heavenly Father,

Nothing is too hard for You. You can—*and will*—handle everything that comes my way, including. . .

Here's what's happening in my life right now. . .

And here's where I need Your reassuring presence, Father. . .

When worries threaten to overwhelm me, please help me to fix my mind on things that truly deserve my focus, like. . .

I trust You to. . .

I leave everything in Your mighty hands, God.

Thank You, Father, for hearing my prayers. *Amen.*

No one can please God without faith. Whoever goes to God must believe that God exists and that he rewards those who seek him.

HEBREWS 11:6 GW

Date:

Dear Heavenly Father,

Nothing is too hard for You. You can—*and will*—handle everything that comes my way, including. . .

Here's what's happening in my life right now. . .

And here's where I need Your reassuring presence, Father. . .

When worries threaten to overwhelm me, please help me to fix my mind on things that truly deserve my focus, like. . .

I trust You to. . .

I leave everything in Your mighty hands, God.

Thank You, Father, for hearing my prayers. *Amen.*

Be not afraid or dismayed at this great multitude;
for the battle is not yours, but God's. . . . You shall not
need to fight in this battle; take your positions, stand still,
and see the deliverance of the Lord [Who is] with you.
2 Chronicles 20:15, 17 ampc

Date:

Dear Heavenly Father,

Nothing is too hard for You. You can—*and will*—handle everything that comes my way, including. . .

Here's what's happening in my life right now. . .

And here's where I need Your reassuring presence, Father. . .

When worries threaten to overwhelm me, please help me to fix my mind on things that truly deserve my focus, like. . .

I trust You to. . .

I leave everything in Your mighty hands, God.

Thank You, Father, for hearing my prayers. *Amen.*

The Lord isn't slow to do what he promised. . . . Rather, he is patient for your sake. He doesn't want to destroy anyone but wants all people to have an opportunity to turn to him and change the way they think and act.

2 PETER 3:9 GW

Date:

Dear Heavenly Father,

Nothing is too hard for You. You can—*and will*—handle everything that comes my way, including. . .

Here's what's happening in my life right now. . .

And here's where I need Your reassuring presence, Father. . .

When worries threaten to overwhelm me, please help me to fix my mind on things that truly deserve my focus, like. . .

I trust You to. . .

I leave everything in Your mighty hands, God.

Thank You, Father, for hearing my prayers. Amen.

Hear this. . .stand still and consider
the wondrous works of God.
Job 37:14 AMPC

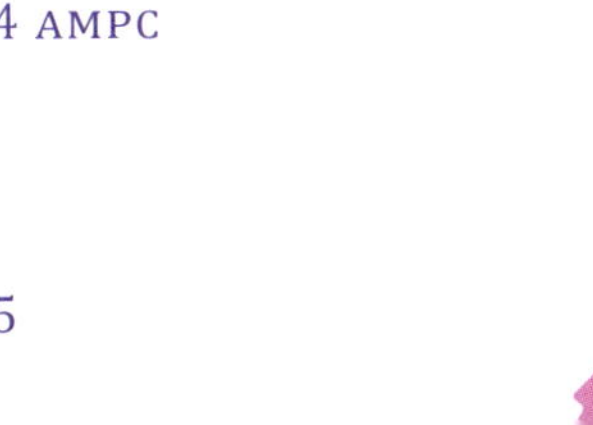

Date:

Dear Heavenly Father,

Nothing is too hard for You. You can—*and will*—handle everything that comes my way, including. . .

Here's what's happening in my life right now. . .

And here's where I need Your reassuring presence, Father. . .

When worries threaten to overwhelm me, please help me to fix my mind on things that truly deserve my focus, like. . .

I trust You to. . .

I leave everything in Your mighty hands, God.

Thank You, Father, for hearing my prayers. *Amen.*

Every day [with its new reasons] will I bless You [affectionately and gratefully praise You]; yes, I will praise Your name forever and ever. . . . On the glorious splendor of Your majesty and on Your wondrous works I will meditate.

Psalm 145:2, 5 AMPC

Date:

Dear Heavenly Father,

Nothing is too hard for You. You can—*and will*—handle everything that comes my way, including. . .

Here's what's happening in my life right now. . .

And here's where I need Your reassuring presence, Father. . .

When worries threaten to overwhelm me, please help me to fix my mind on things that truly deserve my focus, like. . .

I trust You to. . .

I leave everything in Your mighty hands, God.

Thank You, Father, for hearing my prayers. Amen.

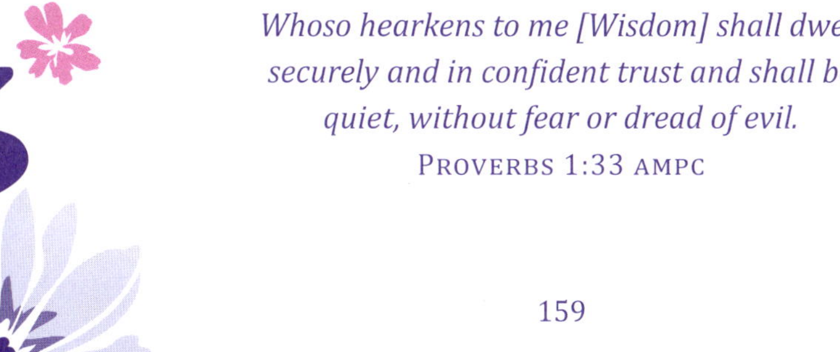

Whoso hearkens to me [Wisdom] shall dwell securely and in confident trust and shall be quiet, without fear or dread of evil.
Proverbs 1:33 AMPC

Date:

Dear Heavenly Father,

Nothing is too hard for You. You can—*and will*—handle everything that comes my way, including. . .

Here's what's happening in my life right now. . .

And here's where I need Your reassuring presence, Father. . .

"I'm convinced: You can do anything and everything. Nothing and no one can upset your plans."
JOB 42:2 MSG

Date:

Dear Heavenly Father,

Nothing is too hard for You. You can—*and will*—handle everything that comes my way, including. . .

Here's what's happening in my life right now. . .

And here's where I need Your reassuring presence, Father. . .

There's one other thing I remember, and remembering,
I keep a grip on hope: God*'s loyal love couldn't have run out,*
his merciful love couldn't have dried up. They're created
new every morning. How great your faithfulness!
Lamentations 3:21–22 msg

Date:

Dear Heavenly Father,

Nothing is too hard for You. You can—*and will*—handle everything that comes my way, including. . .

Here's what's happening in my life right now. . .

And here's where I need Your reassuring presence, Father. . .

When worries threaten to overwhelm me, please help me to fix my mind on things that truly deserve my focus, like. . .

I trust You to. . .

I leave everything in Your mighty hands, God.

Thank You, Father, for hearing my prayers. *Amen.*

Is anyone crying for help?
God is listening, ready to rescue you.
Psalm 34:17 msg

Date:

Dear Heavenly Father,

Nothing is too hard for You. You can—*and will*—handle everything that comes my way, including. . .

Here's what's happening in my life right now. . .

And here's where I need Your reassuring presence, Father. . .

When worries threaten to overwhelm me, please help me to fix my mind on things that truly deserve my focus, like. . .

I trust You to. . .

I leave everything in Your mighty hands, God.

Thank You, Father, for hearing my prayers. *Amen.*

Remember what you said to me, your servant—I hang on to these words for dear life! These words hold me up in bad times; yes, your promises rejuvenate me.
Psalm 119:49–50 msg

Date:

Dear Heavenly Father,

Nothing is too hard for You. You can—*and will*—handle everything that comes my way, including. . .

Here's what's happening in my life right now. . .

And here's where I need Your reassuring presence, Father. . .

I pray that your hearts will be flooded with light so that you can understand the confident hope he has given to those he called.

Ephesians 1:18 NLT

Section 4: When You're Going through a Difficult Time

LAY IT AT THE CROSS

"Come to me, all you who are weary and burdened, and I will give you rest. Take my yoke upon you and learn from me. . .you will find rest for your souls. For my yoke is easy and my burden is light."
MATTHEW 11:28–30 NIV

Does life sometimes get you down? Often when we experience difficulties that weigh us down, we hear the old adage "Lay it at the cross." But how do we lay our difficulties at the cross?

Jesus gives us step-by-step guidance in how to place our difficulties and burdens at the foot of the cross. First, He invites us to come to Him; those of us who are weary and burdened just need to approach Jesus in prayer. Second, He exchanges our heavy and burdensome load with His easy and light load. Jesus gives us His yoke and encourages us to learn from Him. The word *yoke* refers to Christ's teachings, Jesus' *way* of living life. As we follow His teachings, we take His yoke in humility and gentleness, surrendering and submitting ourselves to His will and ways for our lives. Finally, we praise God for the rest He promises to provide us.

Do you have any difficulties in life, any burdens, worries, fears, relationship issues, finance troubles, or work problems that you need to "lay at the cross"? Jesus says, "Come."

Lord, thank You for inviting me to come and exchange my heavy burden for Your light burden. I praise You for the rest You promise me. Amen.

Date:

Dear Heavenly Father,

Today my heart is troubled because. . .

(but with You by my side,
I am comforted!)

I'm feeling. . .

I need Your peace. . .

Even when life is difficult, You provide many blessings, including. . .

Thank You, Father, for hearing my prayers. *Amen.*

As for God, his way is perfect: The LORD's word is flawless; he shields all who take refuge in him.

PSALM 18:30 NIV

Date:

Dear Heavenly Father,

Today my heart is troubled because...

(but with You by my side,
I am comforted!)

I'm feeling...

I need Your peace. . .

Even when life is difficult, You provide many blessings, including. . .

Thank You, Father, for hearing my prayers. *Amen.*

He tends his flock like a shepherd:
He gathers the lambs in his arms and
carries them close to his heart.
Isaiah 40:11 niv

Date:

Dear Heavenly Father,

Today my heart is troubled because. . .

(but with You by my side, I am comforted!)

I'm feeling. . .

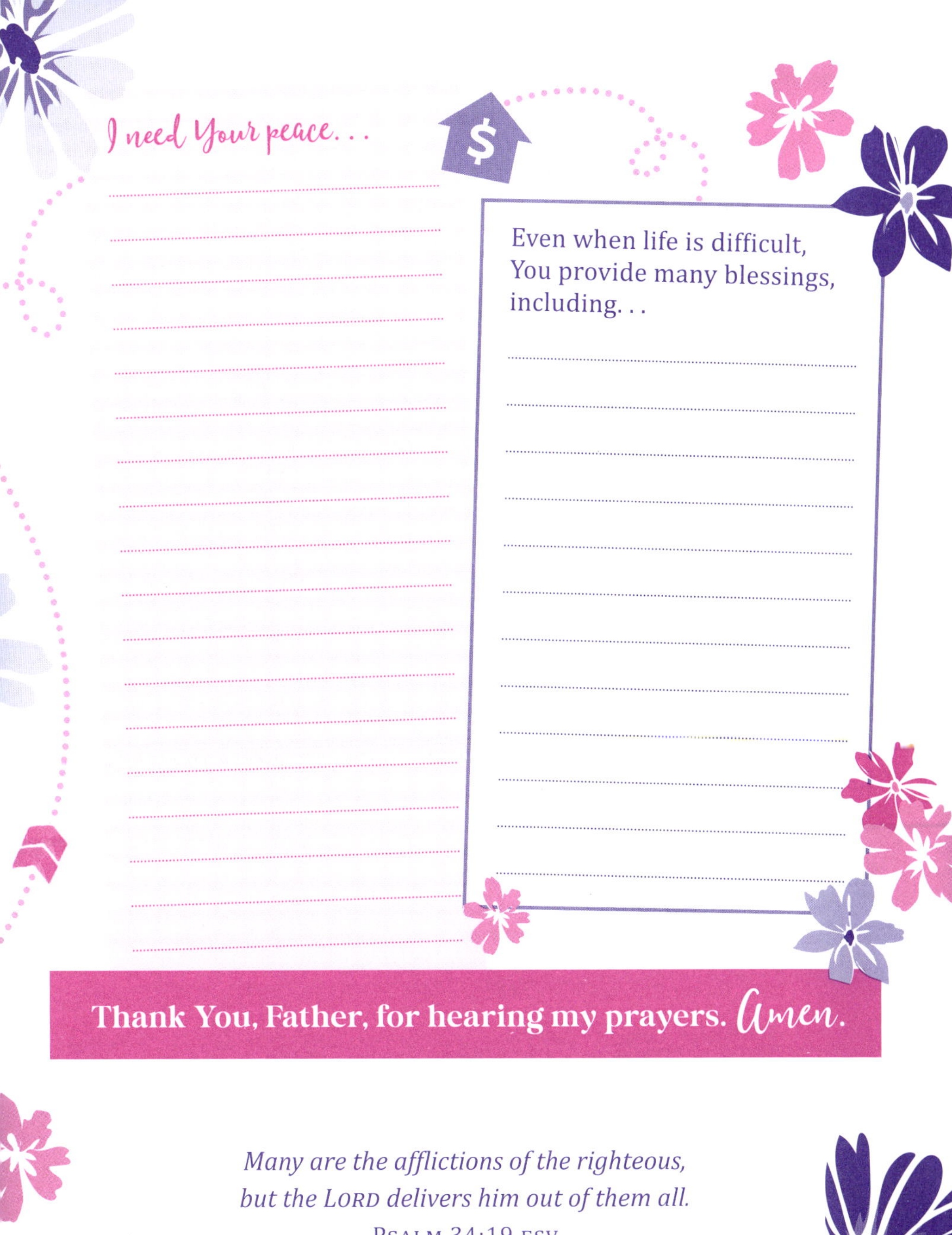

I need Your peace. . .

Even when life is difficult, You provide many blessings, including. . .

Thank You, Father, for hearing my prayers. *Amen.*

Many are the afflictions of the righteous,
but the Lord delivers him out of them all.
Psalm 34:19 ESV

Date:

Dear Heavenly Father,

Today my heart is troubled because. . .

(but with You by my side,
I am comforted!)

I'm feeling. . .

Thank You, Father, for hearing my prayers. *Amen.*

"You, Lord, are my lamp; the Lord turns my darkness into light."
2 Samuel 22:29 niv

Date:

Dear Heavenly Father,

Today my heart is troubled because. . .

(but with You by my side, I am comforted!)

I'm feeling. . .

I need Your peace. . .

Even when life is difficult, You provide many blessings, including. . .

Thank You, Father, for hearing my prayers. Amen.

"Let not your heart be troubled."
JOHN 14:1 NKJV

Date:

Dear Heavenly Father,

Today my heart is troubled because. . .

(but with You by my side,
I am comforted!)

I'm feeling. . .

I need Your peace. . .

Even when life is difficult, You provide many blessings, including. . .

Thank You, Father, for hearing my prayers. *Amen.*

For he will save the needy when he cries for help,
the afflicted also, and him who has no helper.
PSALM 72:12 NASB

Date:

Dear Heavenly Father,

Today my heart is troubled because...

(but with You by my side,
I am comforted!)

I'm feeling...

I need Your peace. . .

Even when life is difficult, You provide many blessings, including. . .

Thank You, Father, for hearing my prayers. *Amen.*

Let us then with confidence draw near to the throne of grace, that we may receive mercy and find grace to help in time of need.
HEBREWS 4:16 ESV

Date:

Dear Heavenly Father,

Today my heart is troubled because. . .

(but with You by my side,
I am comforted!)

I'm feeling. . .

I need Your peace. . .

Even when life is difficult, You provide many blessings, including. . .

Thank You, Father, for hearing my prayers. *Amen.*

The Lord's unfailing love surrounds the one who trusts in him.
Psalm 32:10 NIV

Date:

Dear Heavenly Father,

Today my heart is troubled because...

(but with You by my side,
I am comforted!)

I'm feeling...

Thank You, Father, for hearing my prayers. *Amen.*

"I have told you these things, so that in me you may have peace. In this world you will have trouble. But take heart! I have overcome the world."

John 16:33 niv

Date:

Dear Heavenly Father,

Today my heart is troubled because. . .

(but with You by my side,
I am comforted!)

I'm feeling. . .

I need Your peace. . .

Even when life is difficult, You provide many blessings, including. . .

Thank You, Father, for hearing my prayers. Amen.

May the God of hope fill you with all joy and peace in believing, so that by the power of the Holy Spirit you may abound in hope.
ROMANS 15:13 ESV

Date:

Dear Heavenly Father,

Today my heart is troubled because. . .

(but with You by my side,
I am comforted!)

I'm feeling. . .

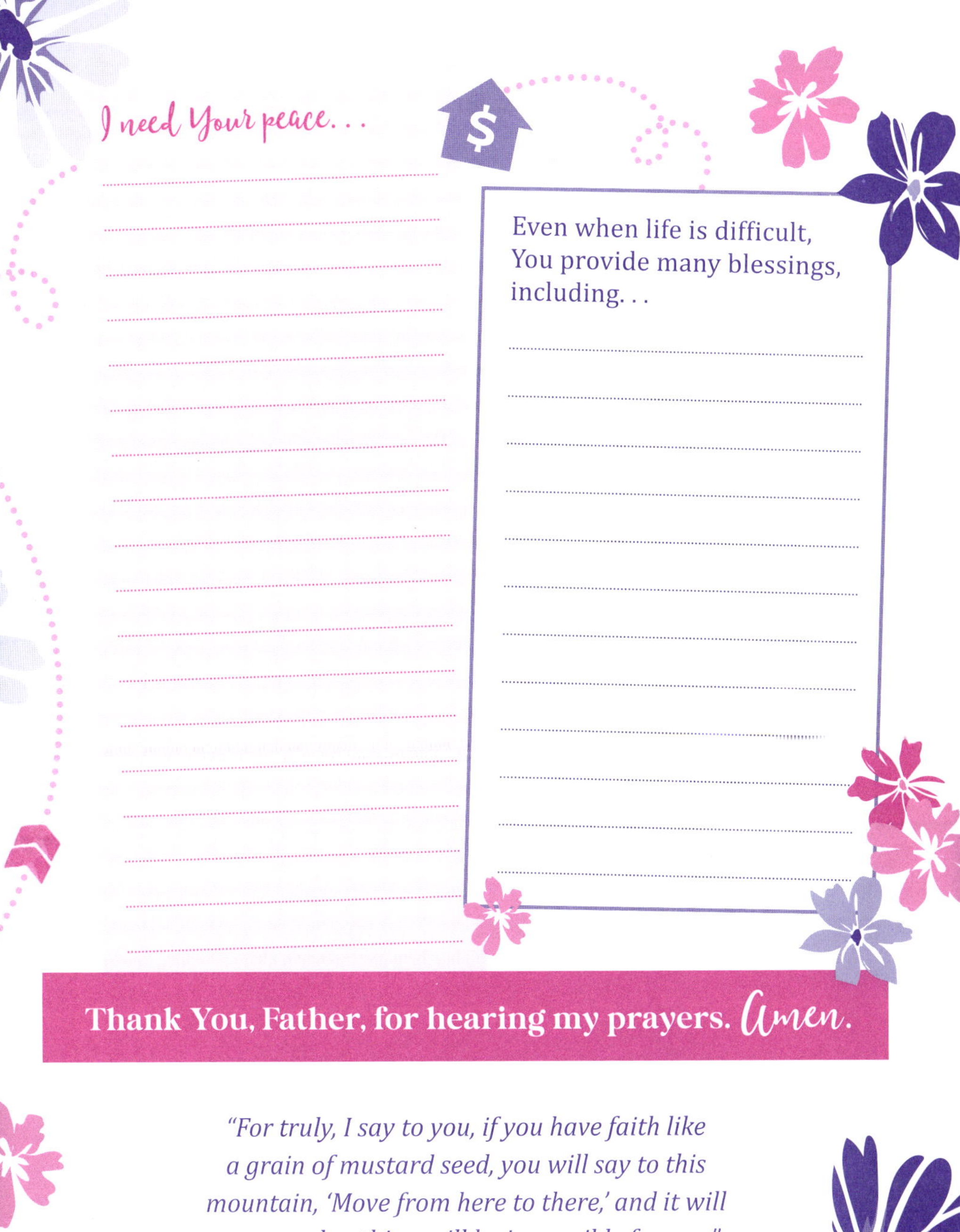

Thank You, Father, for hearing my prayers. *Amen.*

"For truly, I say to you, if you have faith like a grain of mustard seed, you will say to this mountain, 'Move from here to there,' and it will move, and nothing will be impossible for you."
Matthew 17:20 ESV

Date:

Dear Heavenly Father,

Today my heart is troubled because...

(but with You by my side,
I am comforted!)

I'm feeling...

I need Your peace. . .

Even when life is difficult, You provide many blessings, including. . .

Thank You, Father, for hearing my prayers. *Amen.*

"Call to me and I will answer you, and will tell you great and hidden things that you have not known."
JEREMIAH 33:3 ESV

Date:

Dear Heavenly Father,

Today my heart is troubled because...

(but with You by my side,
I am comforted!)

I'm feeling...

I need Your peace. . .

Even when life is difficult, You provide many blessings, including. . .

Thank You, Father, for hearing my prayers. *Amen.*

The LORD is a refuge for the oppressed,
a stronghold in times of trouble.
PSALM 9:9 NIV

Date:

Dear Heavenly Father,

Today my heart is troubled because. . .

(but with You by my side,
I am comforted!)

I'm feeling. . .

I need Your peace. . .

Even when life is difficult, You provide many blessings, including. . .

Thank You, Father, for hearing my prayers. *Amen.*

God has said, "I will never leave you;
I will never abandon you."
HEBREWS 13:5 NCV

Date:

Dear Heavenly Father,

Today my heart is troubled because...

(but with You by my side,
I am comforted!)

I'm feeling...

I need Your peace. . .

Even when life is difficult, You provide many blessings, including. . .

Thank You, Father, for hearing my prayers. *Amen.*

The Lord makes firm the steps of the one who delights in him; though he may stumble, he will not fall, for the Lord upholds him with his hand.

Psalm 37:23–24 niv

Date:

Dear Heavenly Father,

Today my heart is troubled because...

(but with You by my side,
I am comforted!)

I'm feeling...

I need Your peace. . .

Even when life is difficult, You provide many blessings, including. . .

Thank You, Father, for hearing my prayers. *Amen.*

But you, Lord, are a shield around me,
my glory, the One who lifts my head high.
Psalm 3:3 niv

Date:

Dear Heavenly Father,

Today my heart is troubled because. . .

(but with You by my side,
I am comforted!)

I'm feeling. . .

I need Your peace. . .

Even when life is difficult, You provide many blessings, including. . .

Thank You, Father, for hearing my prayers. *Amen.*

Be joyful in hope, patient in affliction, faithful in prayer.
ROMANS 12:12 NIV

Date:

Dear Heavenly Father,

Today my heart is troubled because. . .

(but with You by my side,
I am comforted!)

I'm feeling. . .

I need Your peace. . .

Even when life is difficult, You provide many blessings, including. . .

Thank You, Father, for hearing my prayers. *Amen.*

He got up, rebuked the wind and said to the waves, "Quiet! Be still!" Then the wind died down and it was completely calm.

MARK 4:39 NIV

Date:

Dear Heavenly Father,

Today my heart is troubled because. . .

(but with You by my side,
I am comforted!)

I'm feeling. . .

I need Your peace. . .

Even when life is difficult, You provide many blessings, including. . .

Thank You, Father, for hearing my prayers. *Amen.*

I called on your name, Lord, from the depths of the pit. You heard my plea: "Do not close your ears to my cry for relief."

Lamentations 3:55–56 niv

Date:

Dear Heavenly Father,

Today my heart is troubled because. . .

(but with You by my side,
I am comforted!)

I'm feeling. . .

I need Your peace. . .

Even when life is difficult, You provide many blessings, including. . .

Thank You, Father, for hearing my prayers. *Amen.*

You, Lord, took up my case;
you redeemed my life.
LAMENTATIONS 3:58 NIV

Date:

Dear Heavenly Father,

Today my heart is troubled because. . .

(but with You by my side,
I am comforted!)

I'm feeling. . .

I need Your peace. . .

Even when life is difficult, You provide many blessings, including. . .

Thank You, Father, for hearing my prayers. *Amen.*

Delight yourselves in God, yes, find your joy in him at all times. Have a reputation for gentleness, and never forget the nearness of your Lord.

PHILIPPIANS 4:4–5 PHILLIPS

Date:

Dear Heavenly Father,

Today my heart is troubled because. . .

(but with You by my side,
I am comforted!)

I'm feeling. . .

I need Your peace. . .

Even when life is difficult, You provide many blessings, including. . .

Thank You, Father, for hearing my prayers. *Amen.*

We can be full of joy here and now even in our trials and troubles. Taken in the right spirit these very things will give us patient endurance; this in turn will develop a mature character, and a character of this sort produces a steady hope, a hope that will never disappoint us.

Romans 5:3–5 PHILLIPS

Date:

Dear Heavenly Father,

Today my heart is troubled because. . .

(but with You by my side,
I am comforted!)

I'm feeling. . .

I need Your peace. . .

Even when life is difficult, You provide many blessings, including. . .

Thank You, Father, for hearing my prayers. *Amen.*

Now all glory to God, who is able, through his mighty power at work within us, to accomplish infinitely more than we might ask or think.

Ephesians 3:20 NLT

Date:

Dear Heavenly Father,

Today my heart is troubled because. . .

(but with You by my side,
I am comforted!)

I'm feeling. . .

I need Your peace. . .

Even when life is difficult, You provide many blessings, including. . .

Thank You, Father, for hearing my prayers. Amen.

Behold, I stand at the door and knock; if anyone hears and listens to and heeds My voice and opens the door, I will come in to him.
Revelation 3:20 AMPC

Date:

Dear Heavenly Father,

Today my heart is troubled because. . .

(but with You by my side,
I am comforted!)

I'm feeling. . .

I need Your peace. . .

Even when life is difficult, You provide many blessings, including. . .

Thank You, Father, for hearing my prayers. *Amen.*

I know that the Lord is great,
that our Lord is greater than all gods.
Psalm 135:5 NIV

Section 5: When You Don't Know What to Pray

HOLY SPIRIT PRAYERS

We do not know how to pray as we should, but the Spirit Himself intercedes for us with groanings too deep for words; and He who searches the hearts knows what the mind of the Spirit is, because He intercedes for the saints according to the will of God.

ROMANS 8:26–27

Many times the burdens and troubles of our lives are too complicated to understand. It's difficult for us to put them into words, let alone know how to pray for what we need. And unless we know someone who has been through similar circumstances, we can feel isolated and alone.

But we can always take comfort in knowing that the Holy Spirit knows, understands, and pleads our case before the throne of God the Father. Our groans become words in the Holy Spirit's mouth, turning our mute prayers into praise and intercession "according to the will of God."

We can be encouraged, knowing that our deepest longings and desires, maybe unknown even to us, are presented before the God who knows us and loves us completely. Our names are engraved on His heart and hands. He never forgets us; He intervenes in all things for our good and His glory.

Father, I thank You for the encouragement these verses bring. May I always be aware of the Holy Spirit's interceding on my behalf.

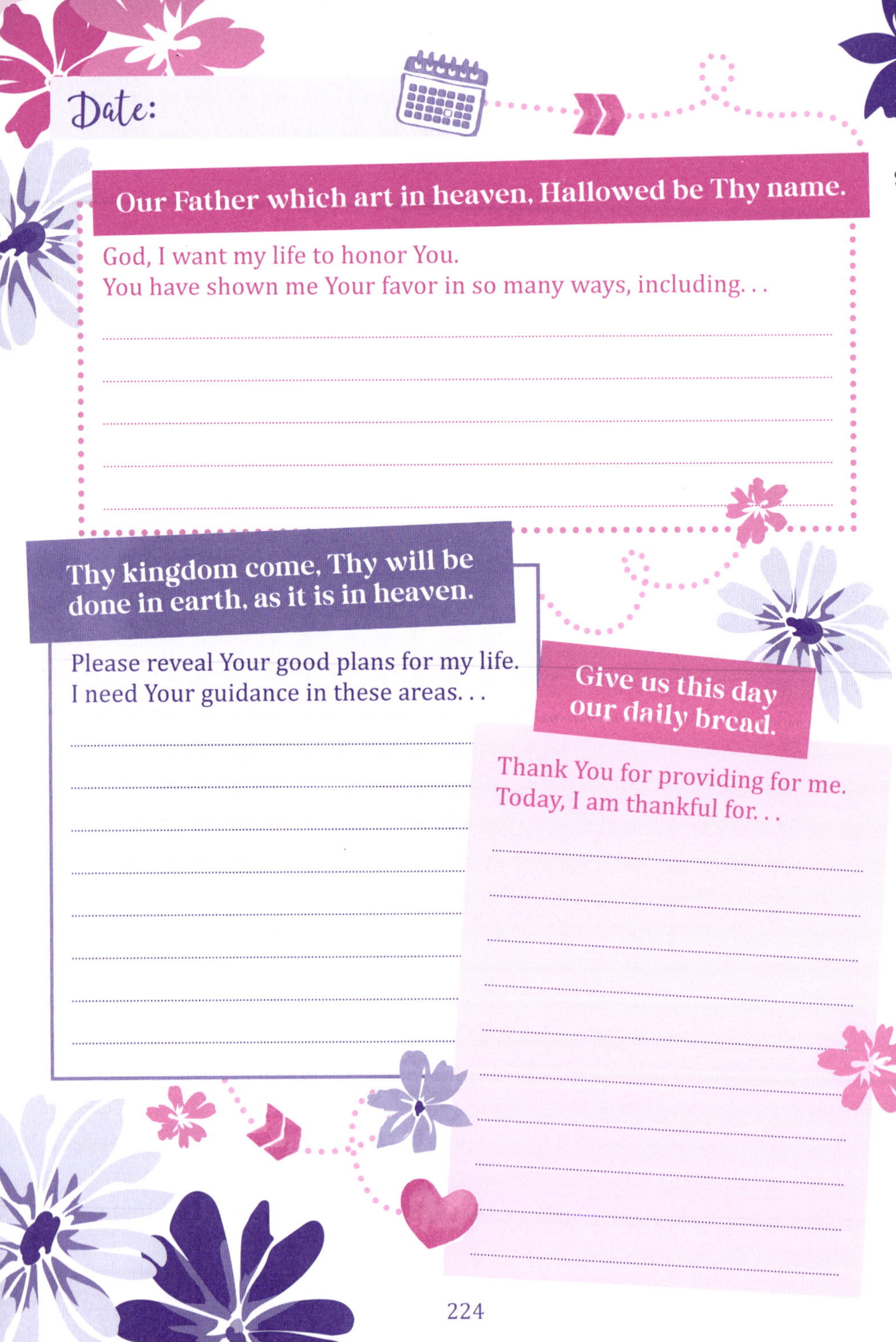

Date:

Our Father which art in heaven, Hallowed be Thy name.

God, I want my life to honor You.
You have shown me Your favor in so many ways, including. . .

Thy kingdom come, Thy will be done in earth, as it is in heaven.

Please reveal Your good plans for my life.
I need Your guidance in these areas. . .

Give us this day our daily bread.

Thank You for providing for me.
Today, I am thankful for. . .

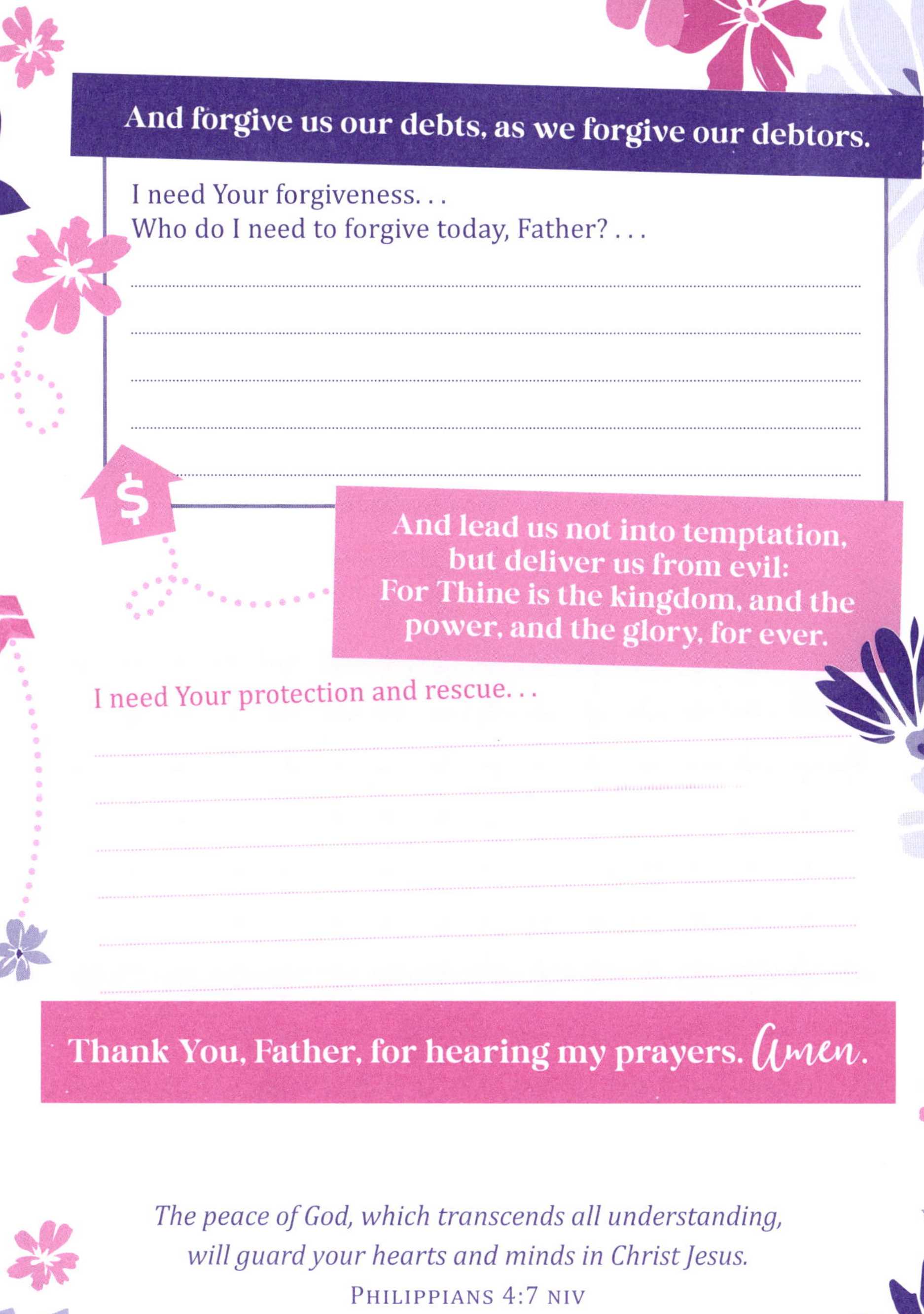

And forgive us our debts, as we forgive our debtors.

I need Your forgiveness. . .
Who do I need to forgive today, Father? . . .

And lead us not into temptation, but deliver us from evil: For Thine is the kingdom, and the power, and the glory, for ever.

I need Your protection and rescue. . .

Thank You, Father, for hearing my prayers. Amen.

The peace of God, which transcends all understanding, will guard your hearts and minds in Christ Jesus.
PHILIPPIANS 4:7 NIV

Date:

Our Father which art in heaven, Hallowed be Thy name.

God, I want my life to honor You.
You have shown me Your favor in so many ways, including. . .

Thy kingdom come, Thy will be done in earth, as it is in heaven.

Please reveal Your good plans for my life.
I need Your guidance in these areas. . .

Give us this day our daily bread.

Thank You for providing for me.
Today, I am thankful for. . .

And forgive us our debts, as we forgive our debtors.

I need Your forgiveness. . .
Who do I need to forgive today, Father? . . .

And lead us not into temptation, but deliver us from evil: For Thine is the kingdom, and the power, and the glory, for ever.

I need Your protection and rescue. . .

Thank You, Father, for hearing my prayers. *Amen*.

Rejoice always. . .for this is the will of God in Christ Jesus for you.
1 Thessalonians 5:16, 18 ESV

Date:

Our Father which art in heaven, Hallowed be Thy name.

God, I want my life to honor You.
You have shown me Your favor in so many ways, including. . .

Thy kingdom come, Thy will be done in earth, as it is in heaven.

Please reveal Your good plans for my life.
I need Your guidance in these areas. . .

Give us this day our daily bread.

Thank You for providing for me.
Today, I am thankful for. . .

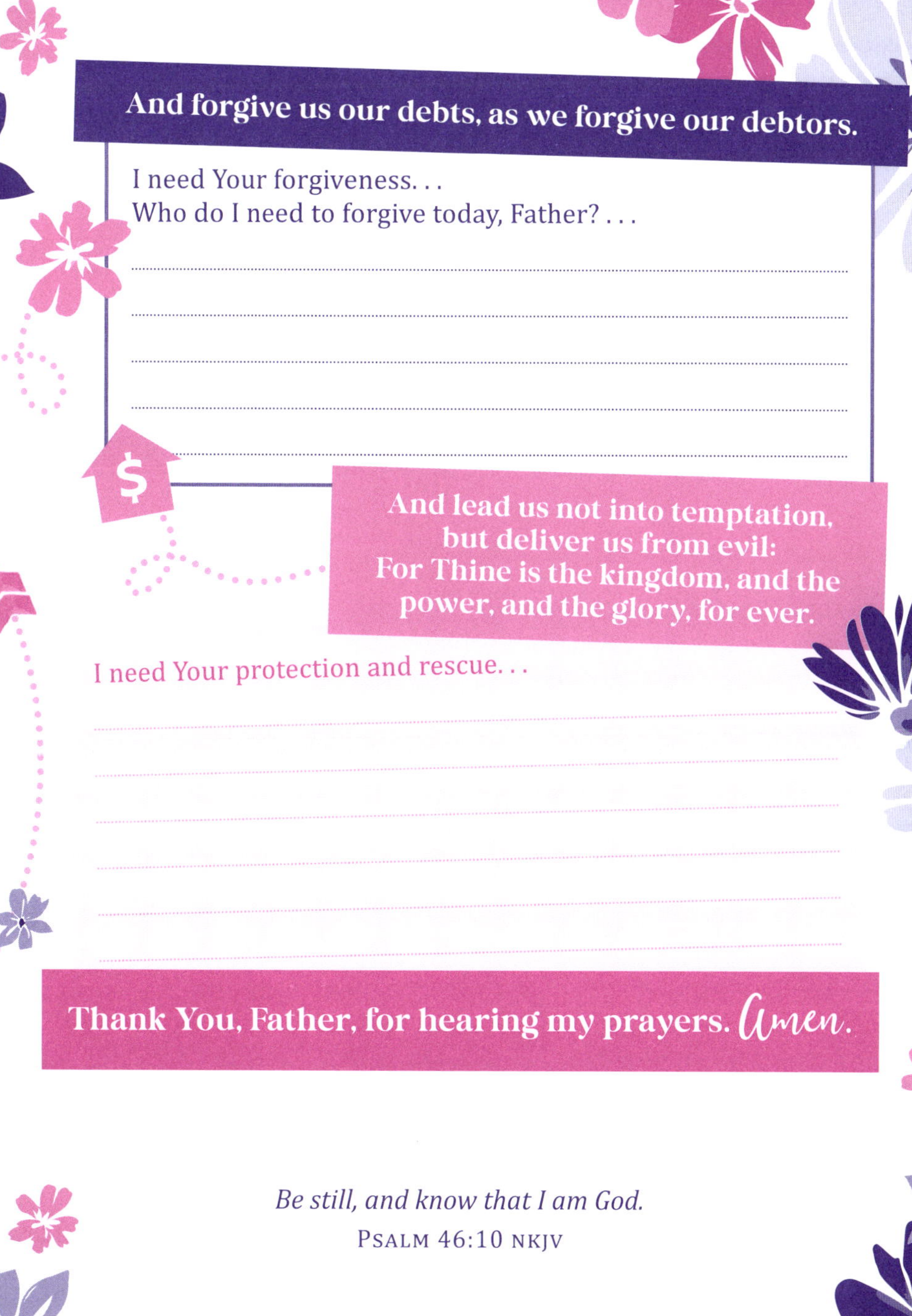

And forgive us our debts, as we forgive our debtors.

I need Your forgiveness. . .
Who do I need to forgive today, Father? . . .

And lead us not into temptation, but deliver us from evil: For Thine is the kingdom, and the power, and the glory, for ever.

I need Your protection and rescue. . .

Thank You, Father, for hearing my prayers. Amen.

Be still, and know that I am God.
PSALM 46:10 NKJV

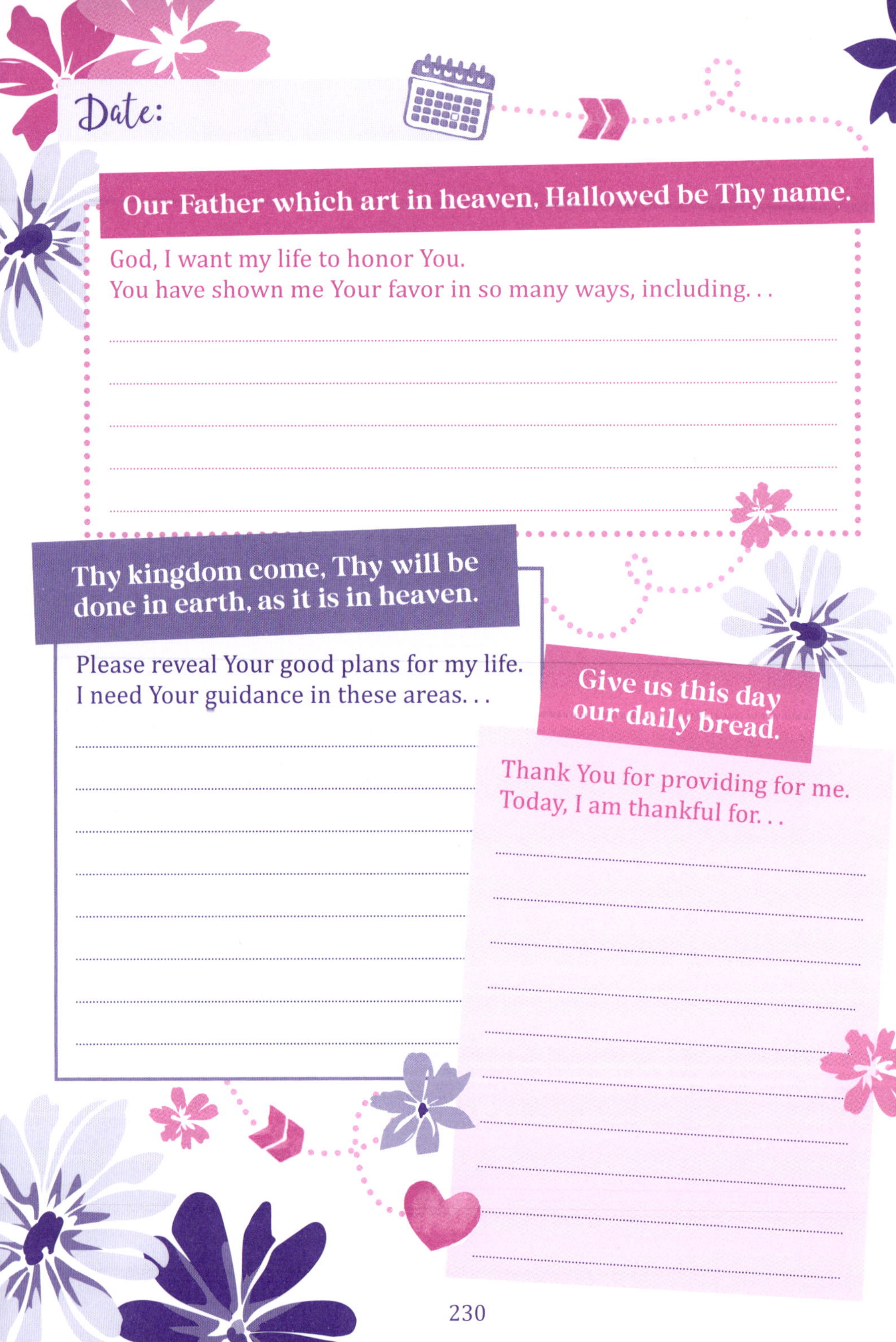

Date:

Our Father which art in heaven, Hallowed be Thy name.

God, I want my life to honor You.
You have shown me Your favor in so many ways, including. . .

Thy kingdom come, Thy will be done in earth, as it is in heaven.

Please reveal Your good plans for my life.
I need Your guidance in these areas. . .

Give us this day our daily bread.

Thank You for providing for me.
Today, I am thankful for. . .

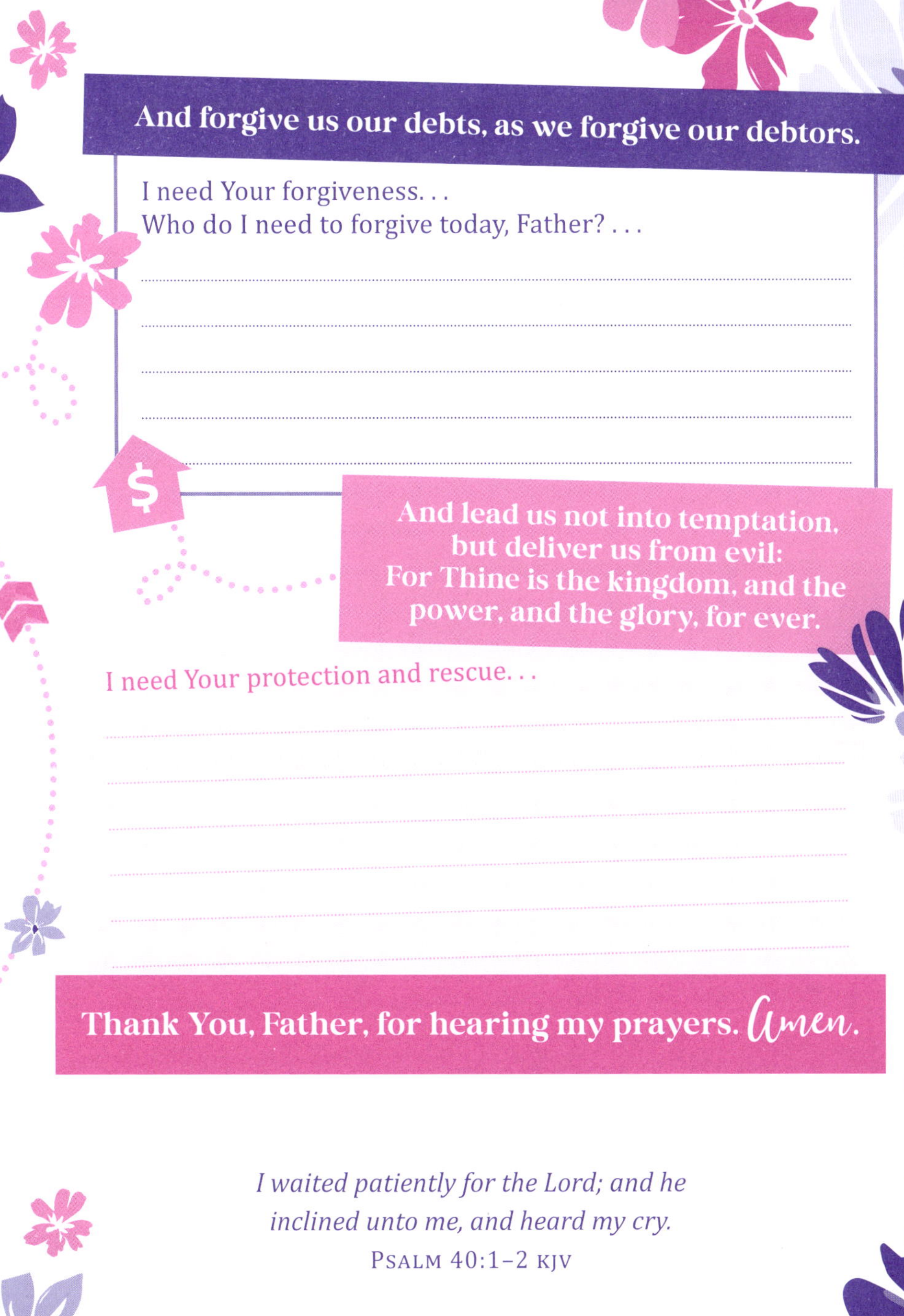

And forgive us our debts, as we forgive our debtors.

I need Your forgiveness. . .
Who do I need to forgive today, Father? . . .

And lead us not into temptation, but deliver us from evil: For Thine is the kingdom, and the power, and the glory, for ever.

I need Your protection and rescue. . .

Thank You, Father, for hearing my prayers. Amen.

I waited patiently for the Lord; and he inclined unto me, and heard my cry.
Psalm 40:1–2 KJV

Date:

Our Father which art in heaven, Hallowed be Thy name.

God, I want my life to honor You.
You have shown me Your favor in so many ways, including. . .

Thy kingdom come, Thy will be done in earth, as it is in heaven.

Please reveal Your good plans for my life.
I need Your guidance in these areas. . .

Give us this day our daily bread.

Thank You for providing for me.
Today, I am thankful for. . .

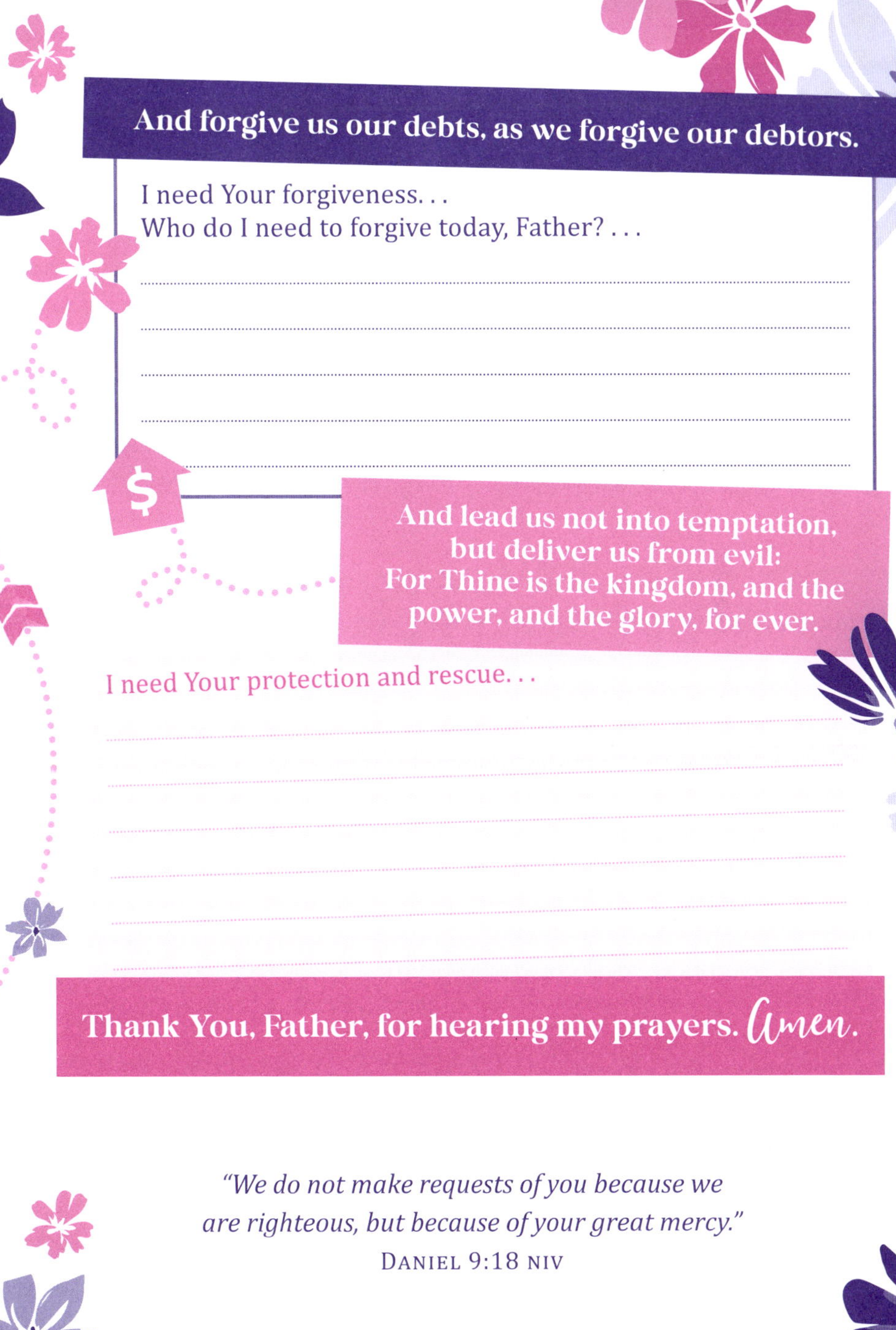

And forgive us our debts, as we forgive our debtors.

I need Your forgiveness. . .
Who do I need to forgive today, Father? . . .

And lead us not into temptation, but deliver us from evil: For Thine is the kingdom, and the power, and the glory, for ever.

I need Your protection and rescue. . .

Thank You, Father, for hearing my prayers. *Amen.*

"We do not make requests of you because we are righteous, but because of your great mercy."
DANIEL 9:18 NIV

Date:

Our Father which art in heaven, Hallowed be Thy name.

God, I want my life to honor You.
You have shown me Your favor in so many ways, including. . .

Thy kingdom come, Thy will be done in earth, as it is in heaven.

Please reveal Your good plans for my life.
I need Your guidance in these areas. . .

Give us this day our daily bread.

Thank You for providing for me.
Today, I am thankful for. . .

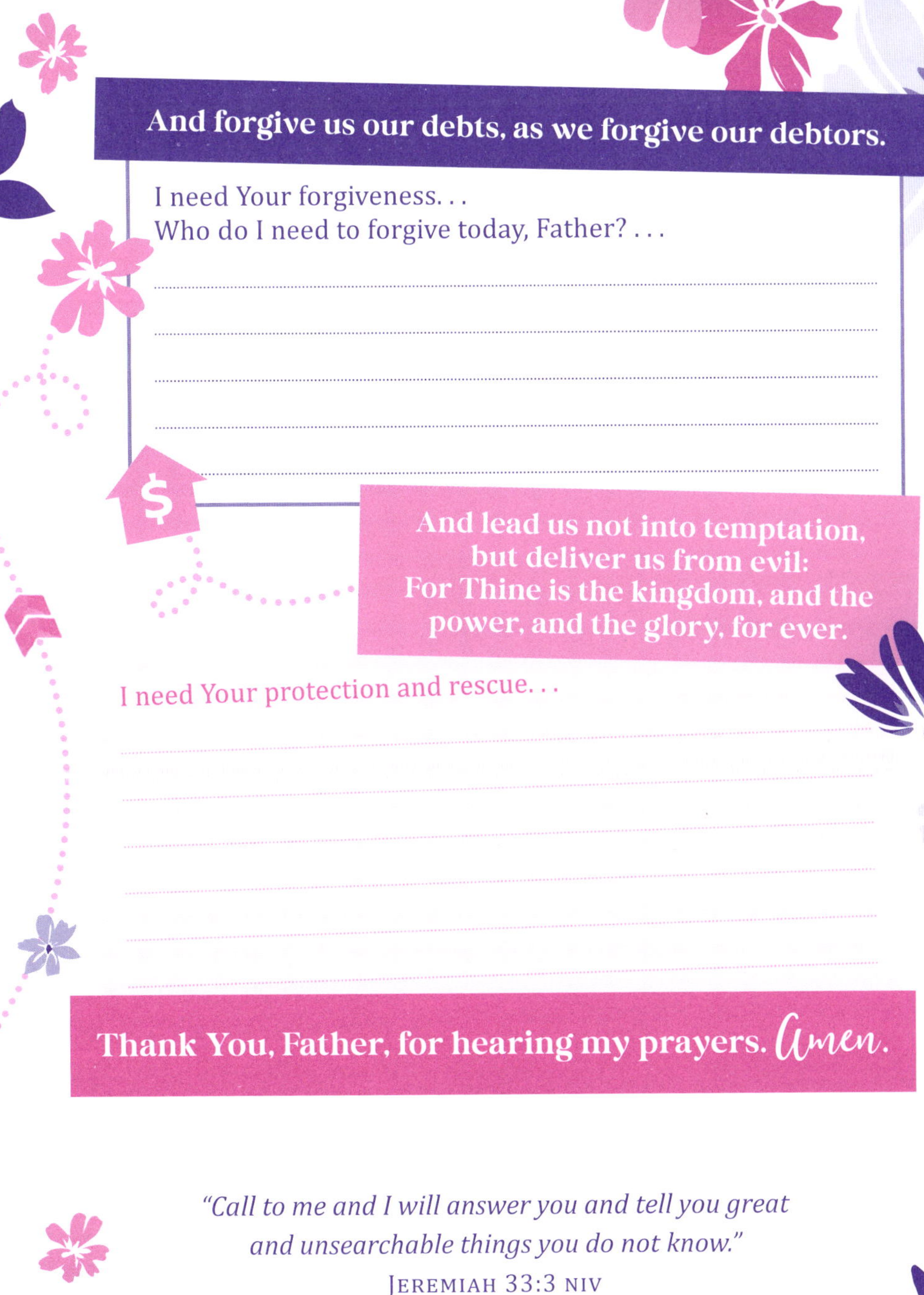

And forgive us our debts, as we forgive our debtors.

I need Your forgiveness. . .
Who do I need to forgive today, Father? . . .

And lead us not into temptation, but deliver us from evil: For Thine is the kingdom, and the power, and the glory, for ever.

I need Your protection and rescue. . .

Thank You, Father, for hearing my prayers. Amen.

"Call to me and I will answer you and tell you great and unsearchable things you do not know."
JEREMIAH 33:3 NIV

Date:

Our Father which art in heaven, Hallowed be Thy name.

God, I want my life to honor You.
You have shown me Your favor in so many ways, including. . .

Thy kingdom come, Thy will be done in earth, as it is in heaven.

Please reveal Your good plans for my life.
I need Your guidance in these areas. . .

Give us this day our daily bread.

Thank You for providing for me.
Today, I am thankful for. . .

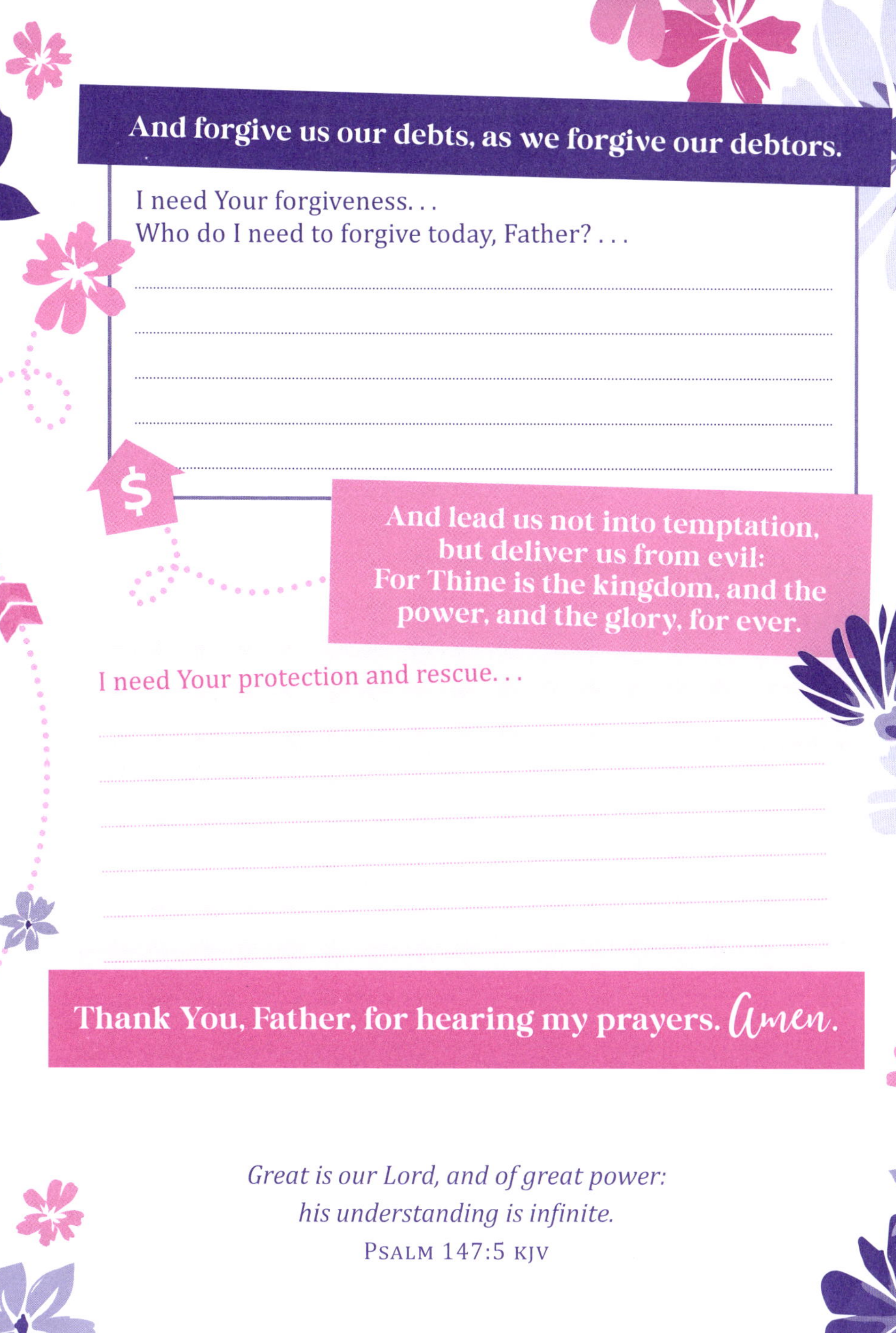

And forgive us our debts, as we forgive our debtors.

I need Your forgiveness. . .
Who do I need to forgive today, Father? . . .

And lead us not into temptation, but deliver us from evil: For Thine is the kingdom, and the power, and the glory, for ever.

I need Your protection and rescue. . .

Thank You, Father, for hearing my prayers. Amen.

Great is our Lord, and of great power:
his understanding is infinite.
PSALM 147:5 KJV

Date:

Our Father which art in heaven, Hallowed be Thy name.

God, I want my life to honor You.
You have shown me Your favor in so many ways, including. . .

Thy kingdom come, Thy will be done in earth, as it is in heaven.

Please reveal Your good plans for my life.
I need Your guidance in these areas. . .

Give us this day our daily bread.

Thank You for providing for me.
Today, I am thankful for. . .

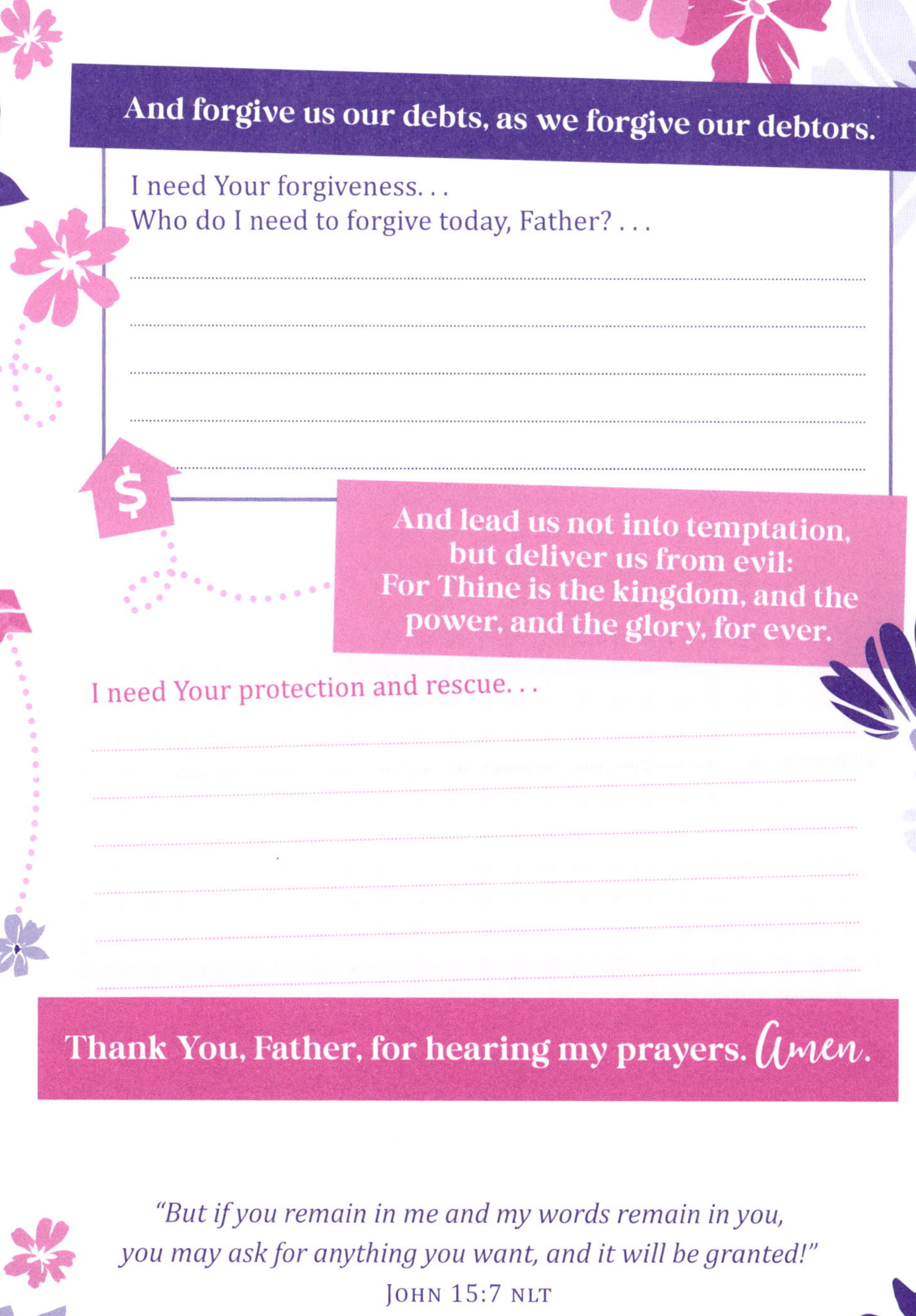

And forgive us our debts, as we forgive our debtors.

I need Your forgiveness. . .
Who do I need to forgive today, Father? . . .

And lead us not into temptation, but deliver us from evil: For Thine is the kingdom, and the power, and the glory, for ever.

I need Your protection and rescue. . .

Thank You, Father, for hearing my prayers. Amen.

"But if you remain in me and my words remain in you, you may ask for anything you want, and it will be granted!"
JOHN 15:7 NLT

Date:

Our Father which art in heaven, Hallowed be Thy name.

God, I want my life to honor You.
You have shown me Your favor in so many ways, including. . .

Thy kingdom come, Thy will be done in earth, as it is in heaven.

Please reveal Your good plans for my life.
I need Your guidance in these areas. . .

Give us this day our daily bread.

Thank You for providing for me.
Today, I am thankful for. . .

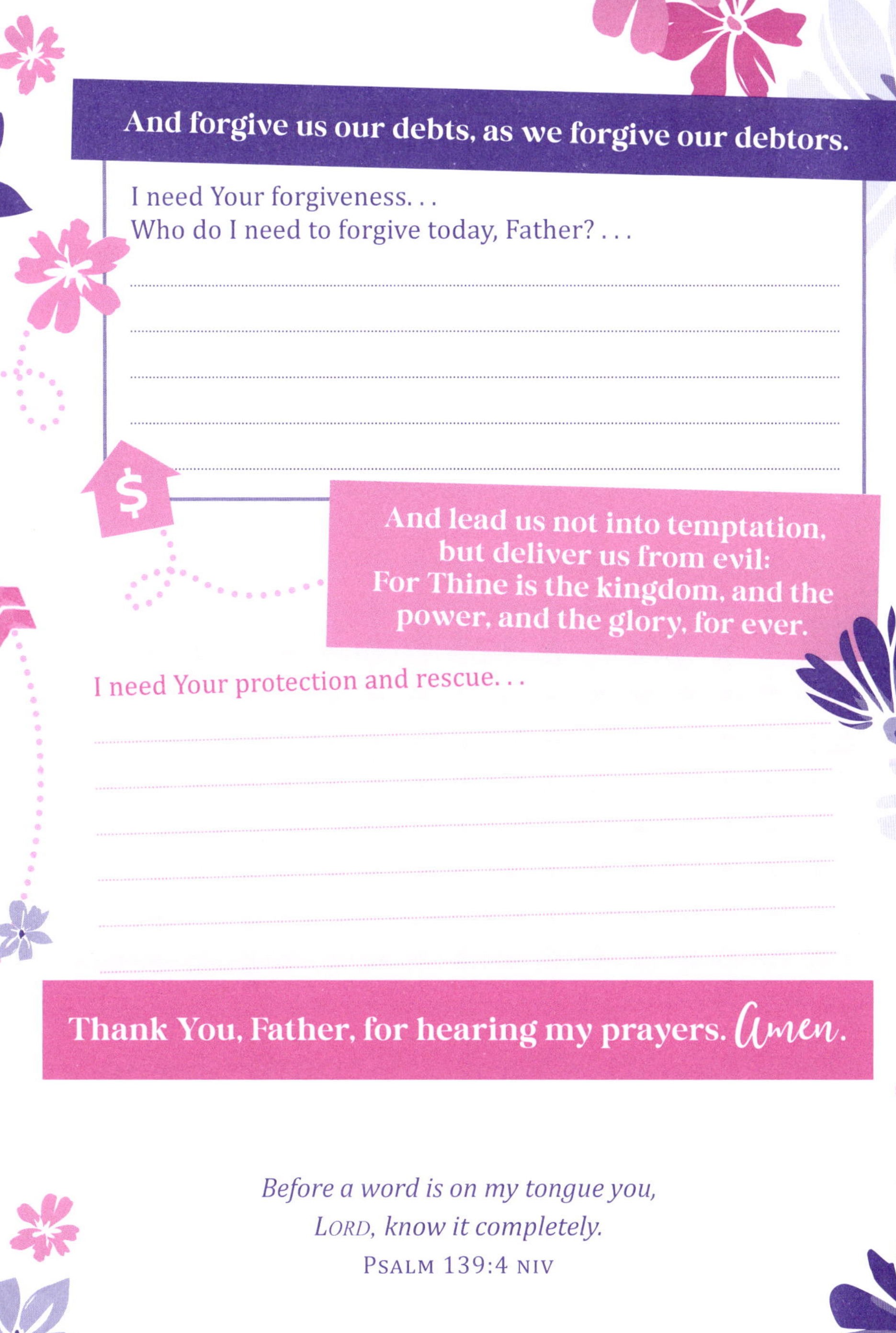

And forgive us our debts, as we forgive our debtors.

I need Your forgiveness. . .
Who do I need to forgive today, Father? . . .

And lead us not into temptation, but deliver us from evil: For Thine is the kingdom, and the power, and the glory, for ever.

I need Your protection and rescue. . .

Thank You, Father, for hearing my prayers. *Amen.*

Before a word is on my tongue you,
Lord, know it completely.
Psalm 139:4 niv

Date:

Our Father which art in heaven, Hallowed be Thy name.

God, I want my life to honor You.
You have shown me Your favor in so many ways, including. . .

Thy kingdom come, Thy will be done in earth, as it is in heaven.

Please reveal Your good plans for my life.
I need Your guidance in these areas. . .

Give us this day our daily bread.

Thank You for providing for me.
Today, I am thankful for. . .

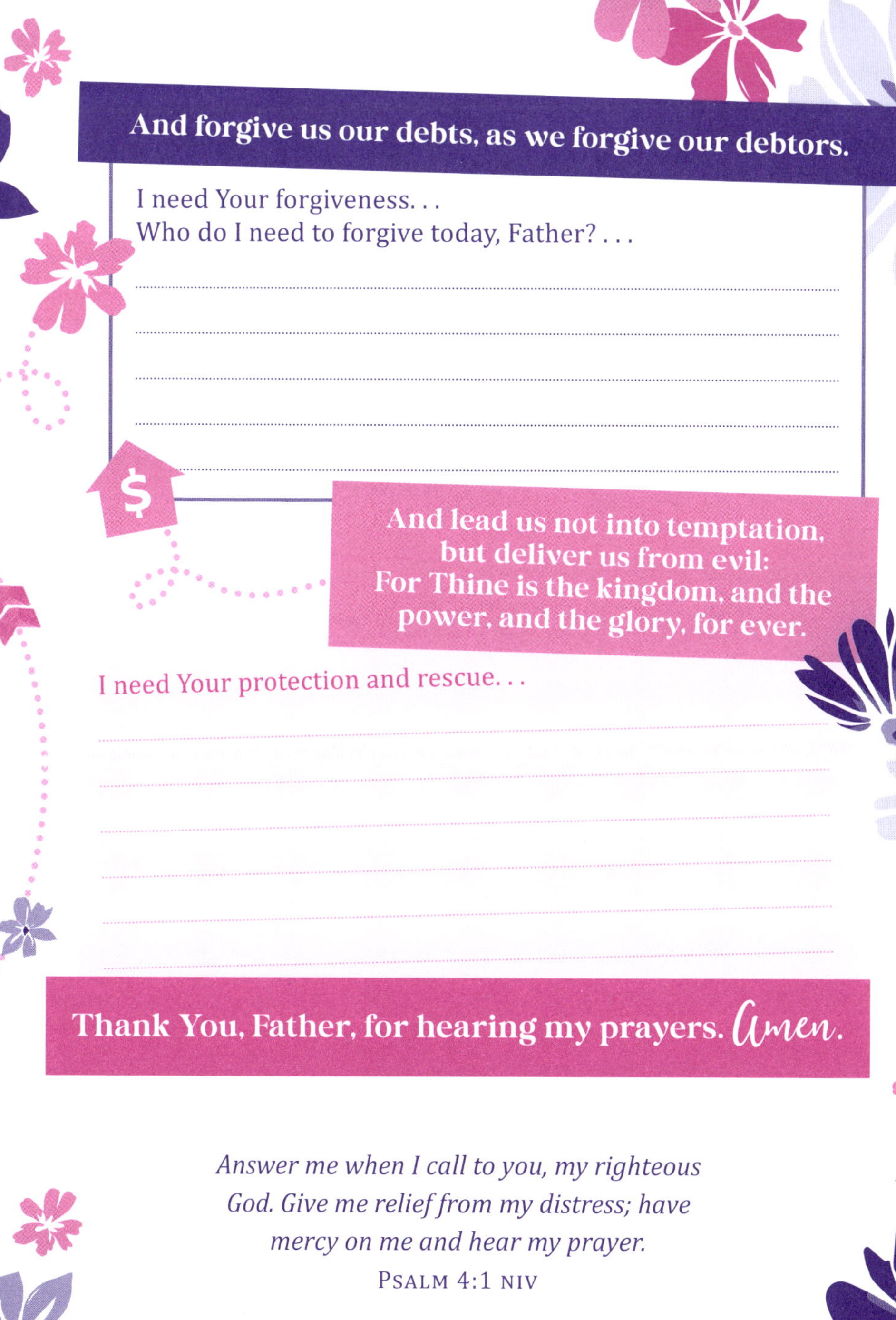

And forgive us our debts, as we forgive our debtors.

I need Your forgiveness. . .
Who do I need to forgive today, Father? . . .

And lead us not into temptation, but deliver us from evil: For Thine is the kingdom, and the power, and the glory, for ever.

I need Your protection and rescue. . .

Thank You, Father, for hearing my prayers. *Amen.*

Answer me when I call to you, my righteous God. Give me relief from my distress; have mercy on me and hear my prayer.

Psalm 4:1 niv

Date:

Our Father which art in heaven, Hallowed be Thy name.

God, I want my life to honor You.
You have shown me Your favor in so many ways, including. . .

Thy kingdom come, Thy will be done in earth, as it is in heaven.

Please reveal Your good plans for my life.
I need Your guidance in these areas. . .

Give us this day our daily bread.

Thank You for providing for me.
Today, I am thankful for. . .

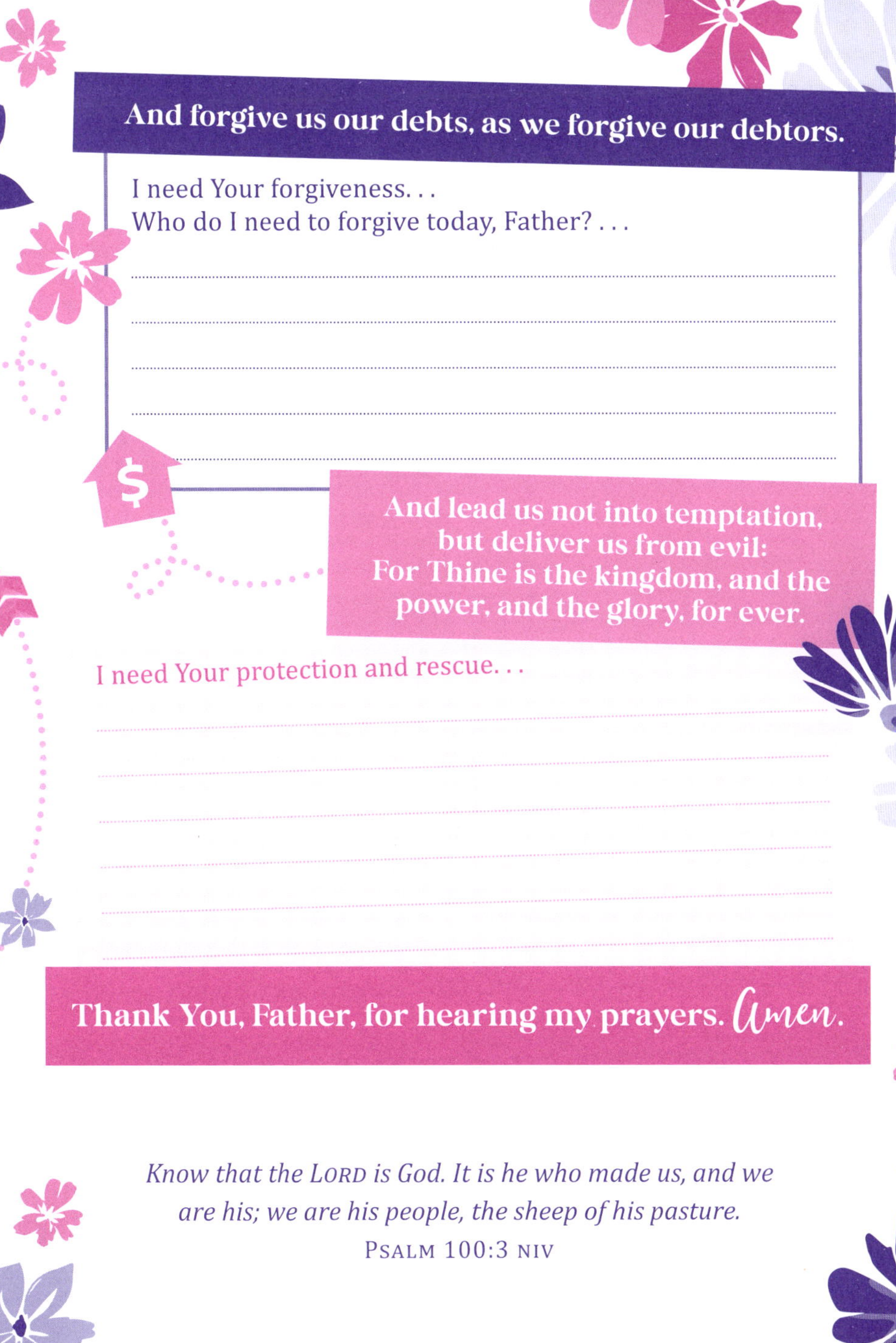

And forgive us our debts, as we forgive our debtors.

I need Your forgiveness. . .
Who do I need to forgive today, Father? . . .

And lead us not into temptation, but deliver us from evil: For Thine is the kingdom, and the power, and the glory, for ever.

I need Your protection and rescue. . .

Thank You, Father, for hearing my prayers. Amen.

Know that the L*ORD is God. It is he who made us, and we are his; we are his people, the sheep of his pasture.*
PSALM 100:3 NIV

Date:

Our Father which art in heaven, Hallowed be Thy name.

God, I want my life to honor You.
You have shown me Your favor in so many ways, including. . .

Thy kingdom come, Thy will be done in earth, as it is in heaven.

Please reveal Your good plans for my life.
I need Your guidance in these areas. . .

Give us this day our daily bread.

Thank You for providing for me.
Today, I am thankful for. . .

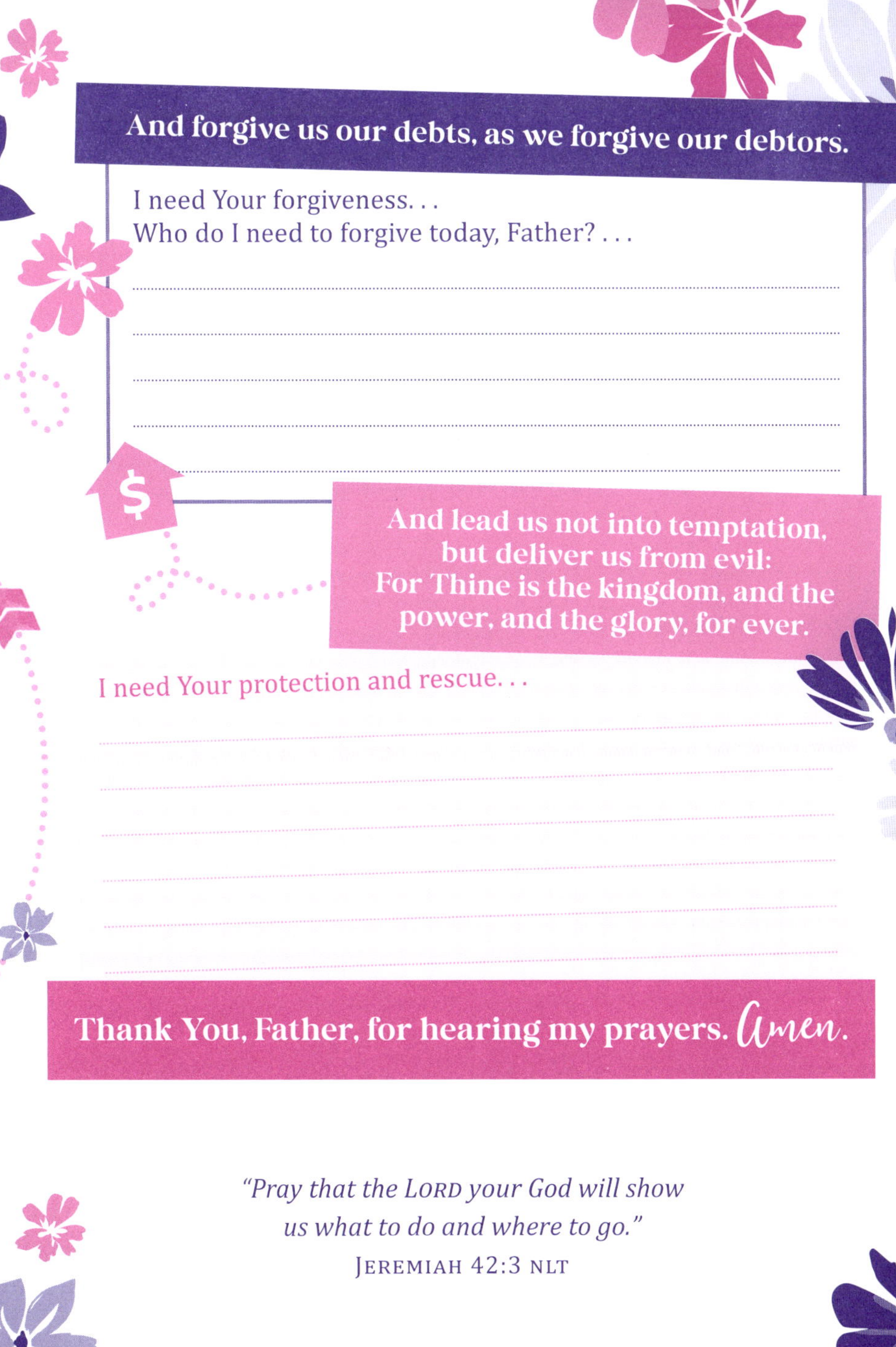

And forgive us our debts, as we forgive our debtors.

I need Your forgiveness. . .
Who do I need to forgive today, Father? . . .

And lead us not into temptation, but deliver us from evil: For Thine is the kingdom, and the power, and the glory, for ever.

I need Your protection and rescue. . .

Thank You, Father, for hearing my prayers. *Amen.*

"Pray that the LORD *your God will show us what to do and where to go."*
JEREMIAH 42:3 NLT

Date:

Our Father which art in heaven, Hallowed be Thy name.

God, I want my life to honor You.
You have shown me Your favor in so many ways, including. . .

Thy kingdom come, Thy will be done in earth, as it is in heaven.

Please reveal Your good plans for my life.
I need Your guidance in these areas. . .

Give us this day our daily bread.

Thank You for providing for me.
Today, I am thankful for. . .

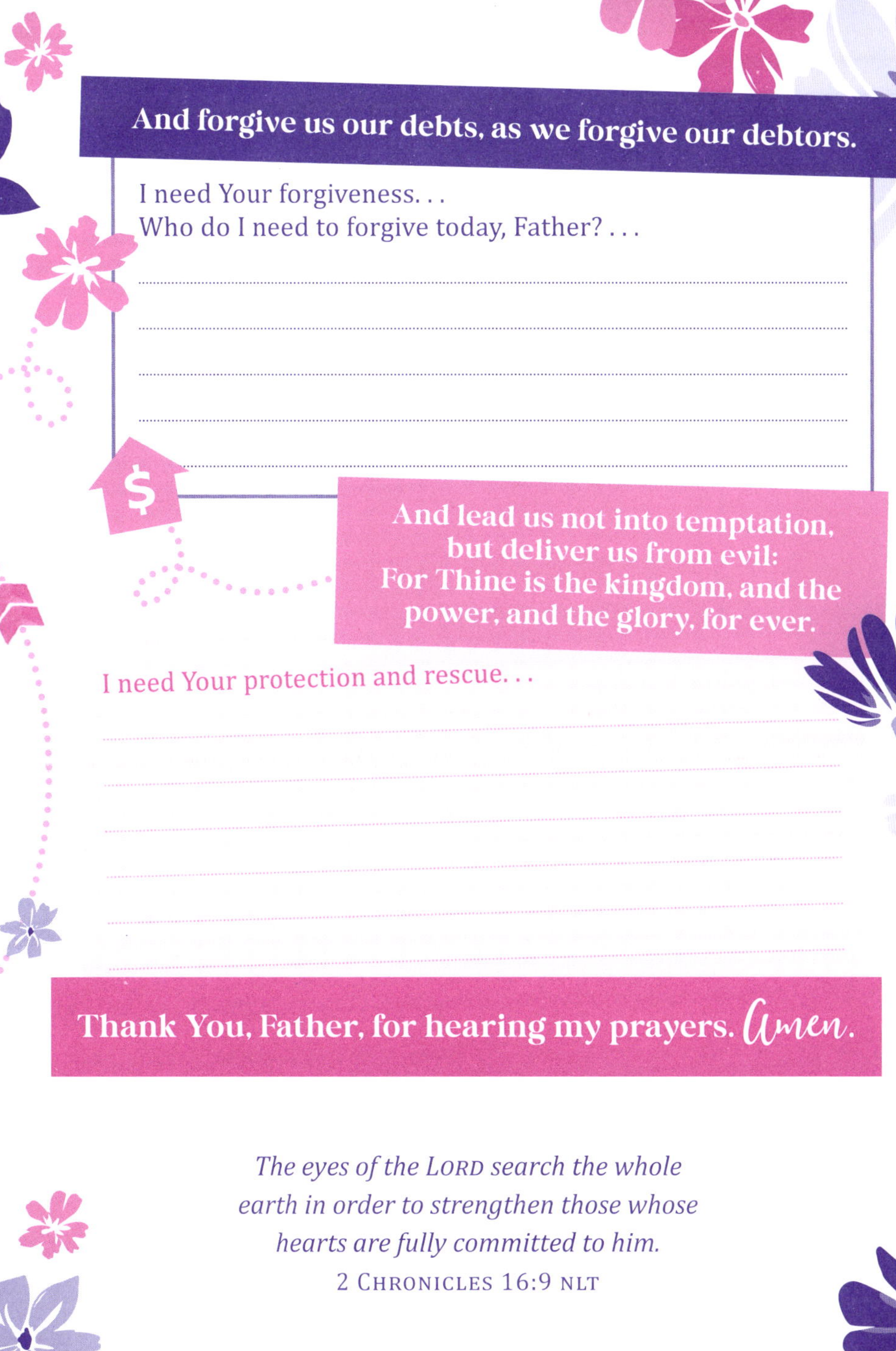

And forgive us our debts, as we forgive our debtors.

I need Your forgiveness. . .
Who do I need to forgive today, Father? . . .

And lead us not into temptation, but deliver us from evil: For Thine is the kingdom, and the power, and the glory, for ever.

I need Your protection and rescue. . .

Thank You, Father, for hearing my prayers. Amen.

The eyes of the Lord search the whole earth in order to strengthen those whose hearts are fully committed to him.
2 Chronicles 16:9 NLT

Date:

Our Father which art in heaven, Hallowed be Thy name.

God, I want my life to honor You.
You have shown me Your favor in so many ways, including. . .

Thy kingdom come, Thy will be done in earth, as it is in heaven.

Please reveal Your good plans for my life.
I need Your guidance in these areas. . .

Give us this day our daily bread.

Thank You for providing for me.
Today, I am thankful for. . .

And forgive us our debts, as we forgive our debtors.

I need Your forgiveness. . .
Who do I need to forgive today, Father? . . .

And lead us not into temptation, but deliver us from evil: For Thine is the kingdom, and the power, and the glory, for ever.

I need Your protection and rescue. . .

Thank You, Father, for hearing my prayers. Amen.

God knows how often I pray for you. Day and night I bring you and your needs in prayer to God.
ROMANS 1:9 NLT

Date:

Our Father which art in heaven, Hallowed be Thy name.

God, I want my life to honor You.
You have shown me Your favor in so many ways, including. . .

Thy kingdom come, Thy will be done in earth, as it is in heaven.

Please reveal Your good plans for my life.
I need Your guidance in these areas. . .

Give us this day our daily bread.

Thank You for providing for me.
Today, I am thankful for. . .

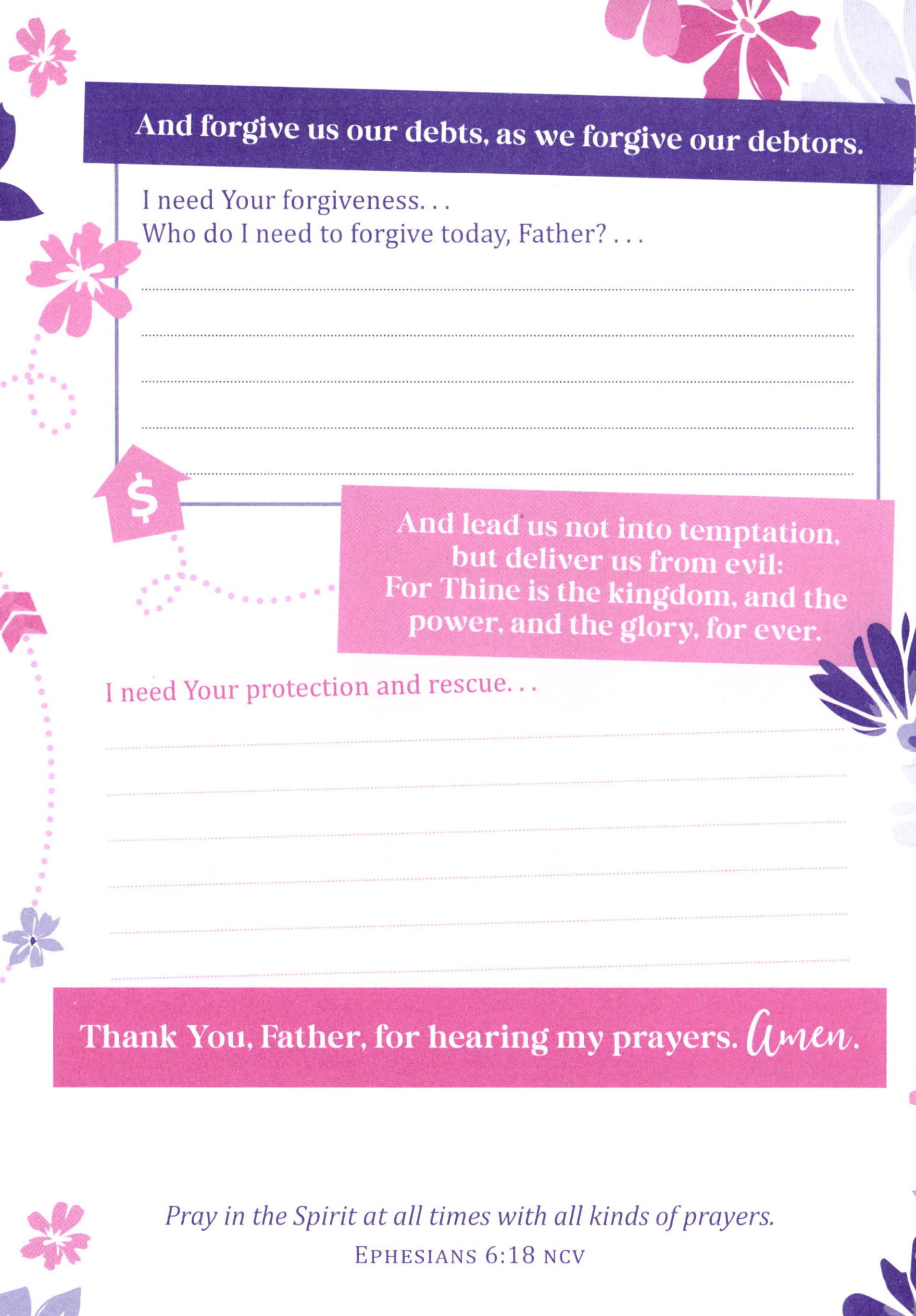

And forgive us our debts, as we forgive our debtors.

I need Your forgiveness. . .
Who do I need to forgive today, Father? . . .

And lead us not into temptation, but deliver us from evil: For Thine is the kingdom, and the power, and the glory, for ever.

I need Your protection and rescue. . .

Thank You, Father, for hearing my prayers. Amen.

Pray in the Spirit at all times with all kinds of prayers.
EPHESIANS 6:18 NCV

Date:

Our Father which art in heaven, Hallowed be Thy name.

God, I want my life to honor You.
You have shown me Your favor in so many ways, including. . .

Thy kingdom come, Thy will be done in earth, as it is in heaven.

Please reveal Your good plans for my life.
I need Your guidance in these areas. . .

Give us this day our daily bread.

Thank You for providing for me.
Today, I am thankful for. . .

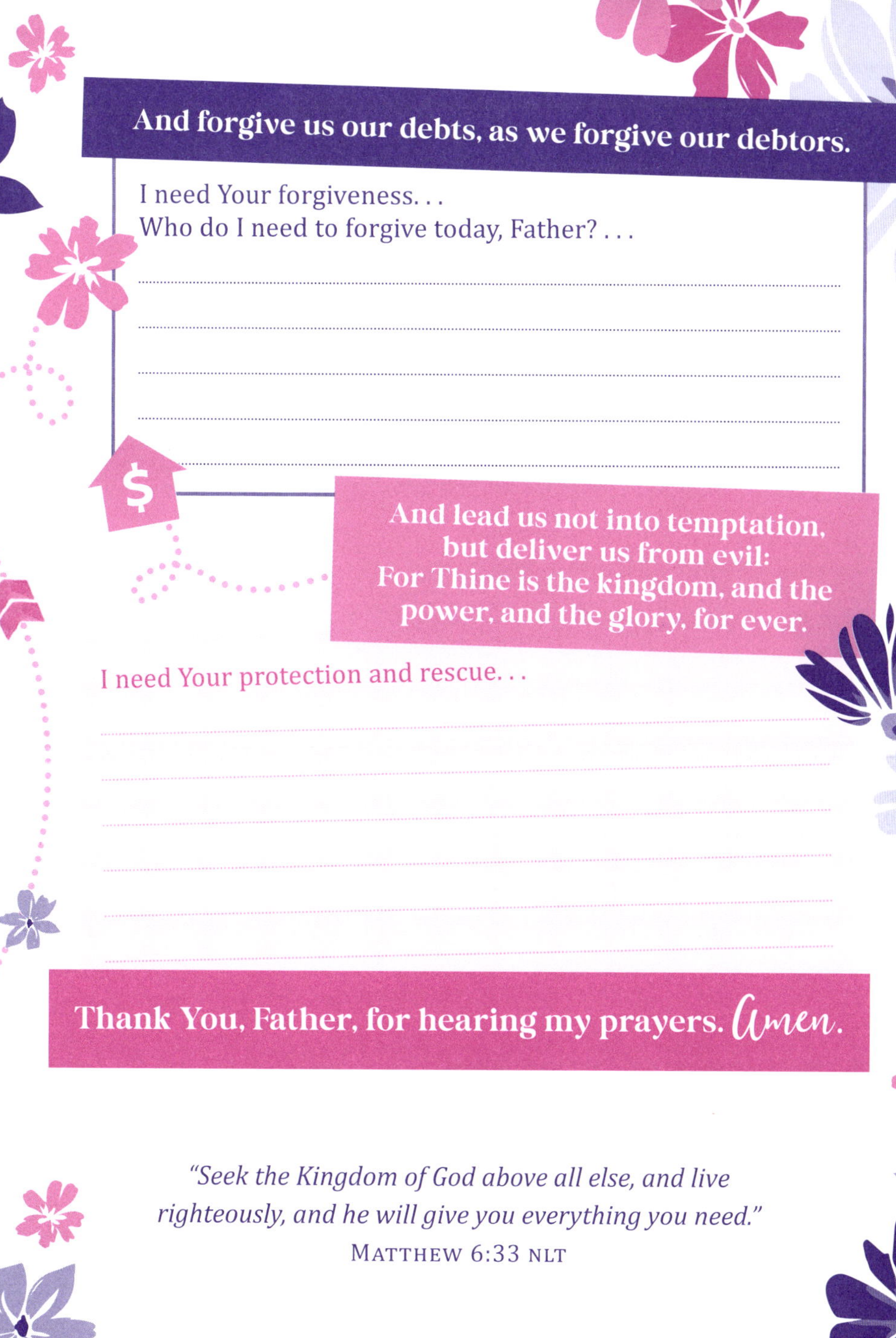

And forgive us our debts, as we forgive our debtors.

I need Your forgiveness. . .
Who do I need to forgive today, Father? . . .

And lead us not into temptation, but deliver us from evil: For Thine is the kingdom, and the power, and the glory, for ever.

I need Your protection and rescue. . .

Thank You, Father, for hearing my prayers. Amen.

"Seek the Kingdom of God above all else, and live righteously, and he will give you everything you need."
MATTHEW 6:33 NLT

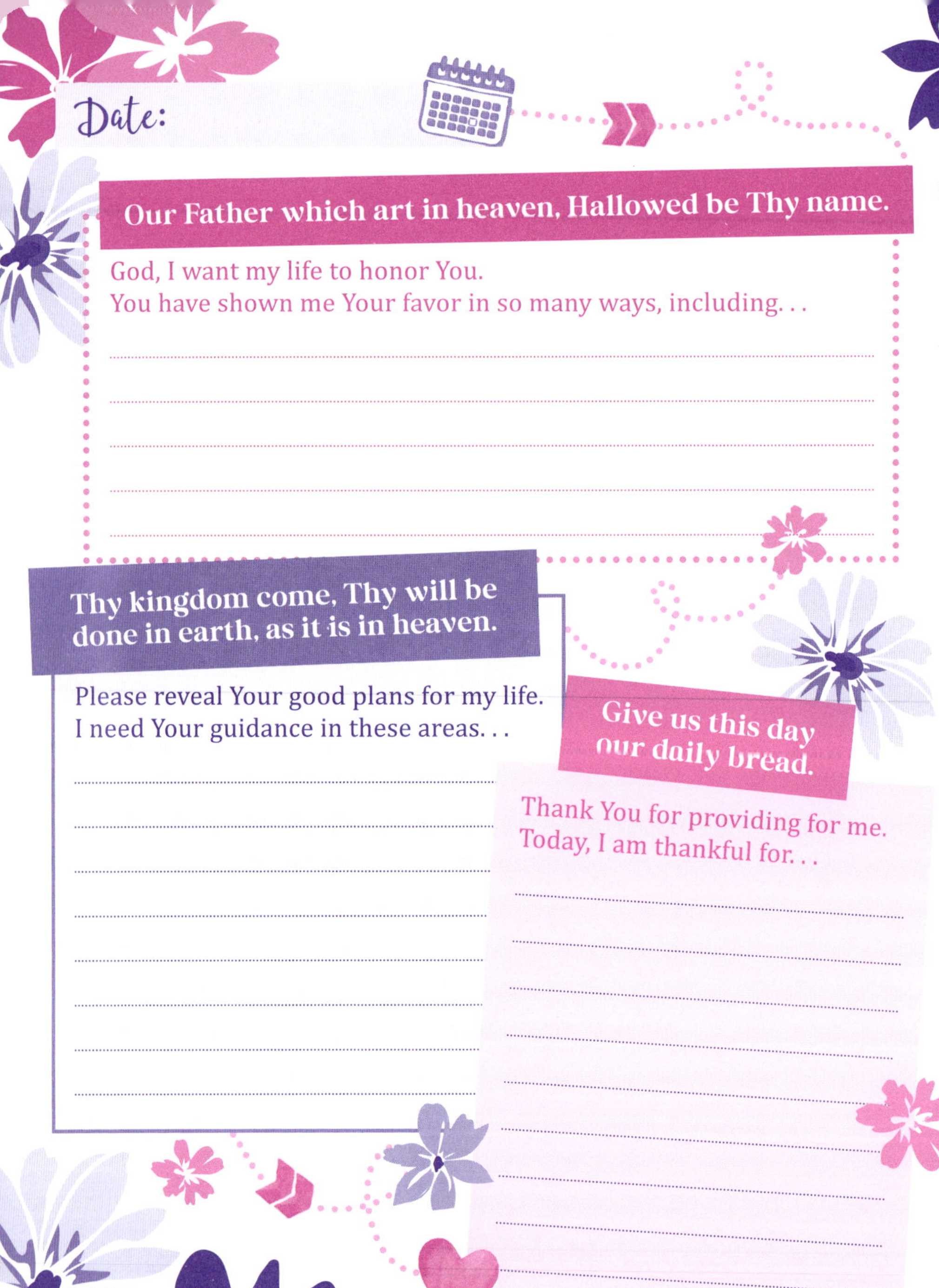

Date:

Our Father which art in heaven, Hallowed be Thy name.

God, I want my life to honor You.
You have shown me Your favor in so many ways, including. . .

Thy kingdom come, Thy will be done in earth, as it is in heaven.

Please reveal Your good plans for my life.
I need Your guidance in these areas. . .

Give us this day our daily bread.

Thank You for providing for me.
Today, I am thankful for. . .

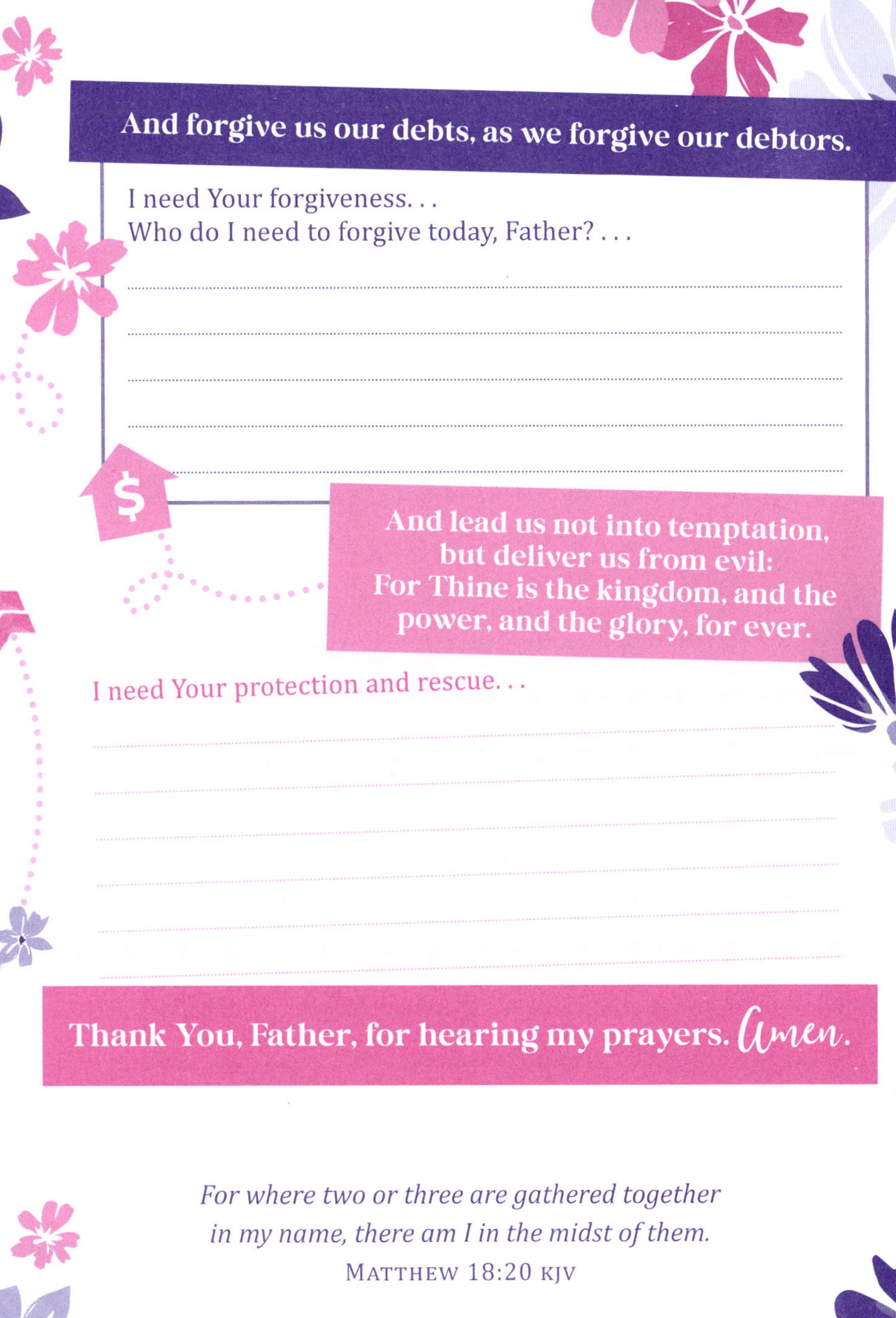

And forgive us our debts, as we forgive our debtors.

I need Your forgiveness. . .
Who do I need to forgive today, Father? . . .

And lead us not into temptation, but deliver us from evil: For Thine is the kingdom, and the power, and the glory, for ever.

I need Your protection and rescue. . .

Thank You, Father, for hearing my prayers. Amen.

For where two or three are gathered together in my name, there am I in the midst of them.
MATTHEW 18:20 KJV

Date:

Our Father which art in heaven, Hallowed be Thy name.

God, I want my life to honor You.
You have shown me Your favor in so many ways, including. . .

Thy kingdom come, Thy will be done in earth, as it is in heaven.

Please reveal Your good plans for my life.
I need Your guidance in these areas. . .

Give us this day our daily bread.

Thank You for providing for me.
Today, I am thankful for. . .

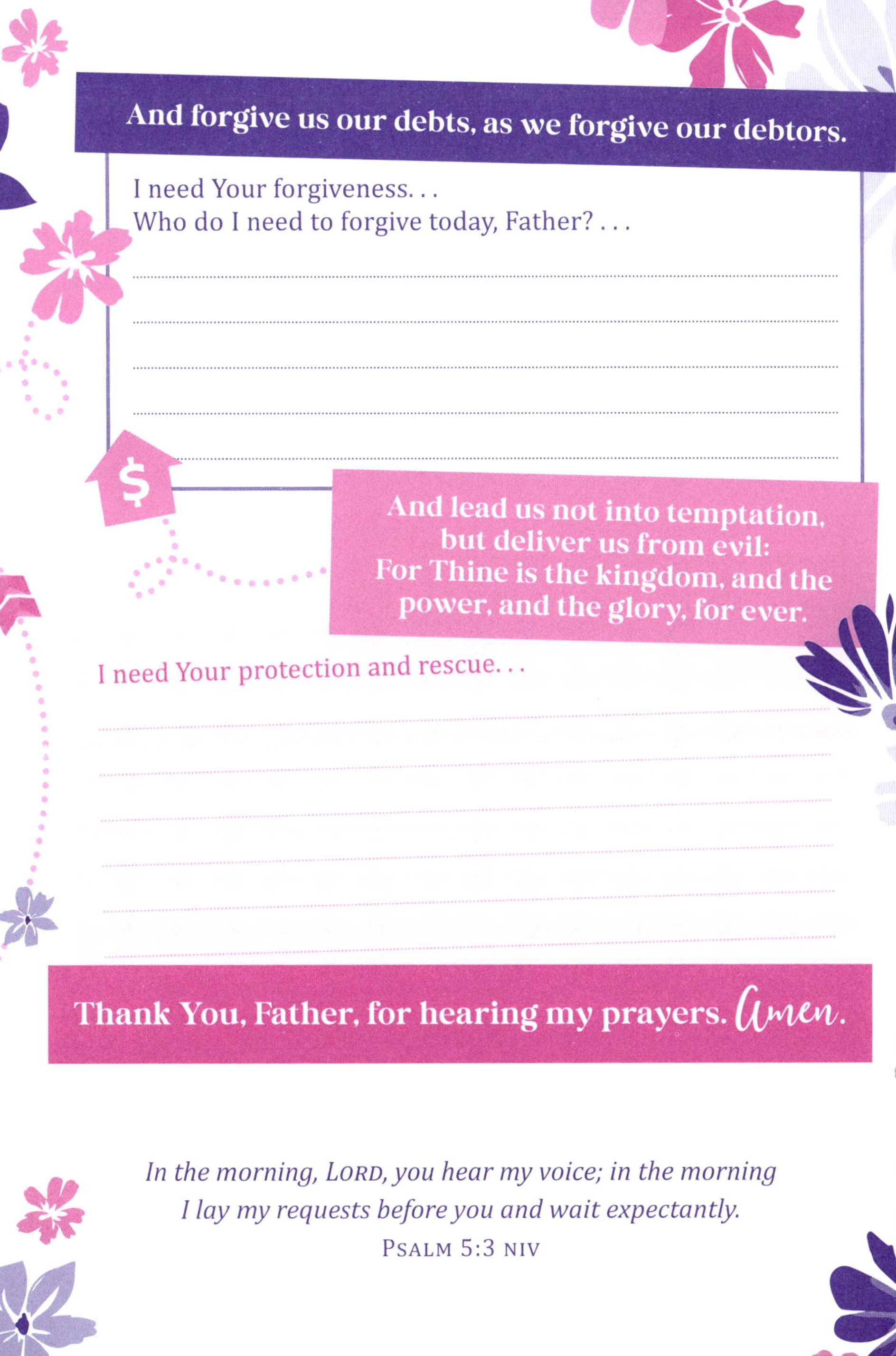

And forgive us our debts, as we forgive our debtors.

I need Your forgiveness. . .
Who do I need to forgive today, Father? . . .

And lead us not into temptation, but deliver us from evil: For Thine is the kingdom, and the power, and the glory, for ever.

I need Your protection and rescue. . .

Thank You, Father, for hearing my prayers. Amen.

In the morning, LORD, you hear my voice; in the morning I lay my requests before you and wait expectantly.
PSALM 5:3 NIV

Date:

Our Father which art in heaven, Hallowed be Thy name.

God, I want my life to honor You.
You have shown me Your favor in so many ways, including. . .

Thy kingdom come, Thy will be done in earth, as it is in heaven.

Please reveal Your good plans for my life.
I need Your guidance in these areas. . .

Give us this day our daily bread.

Thank You for providing for me.
Today, I am thankful for. . .

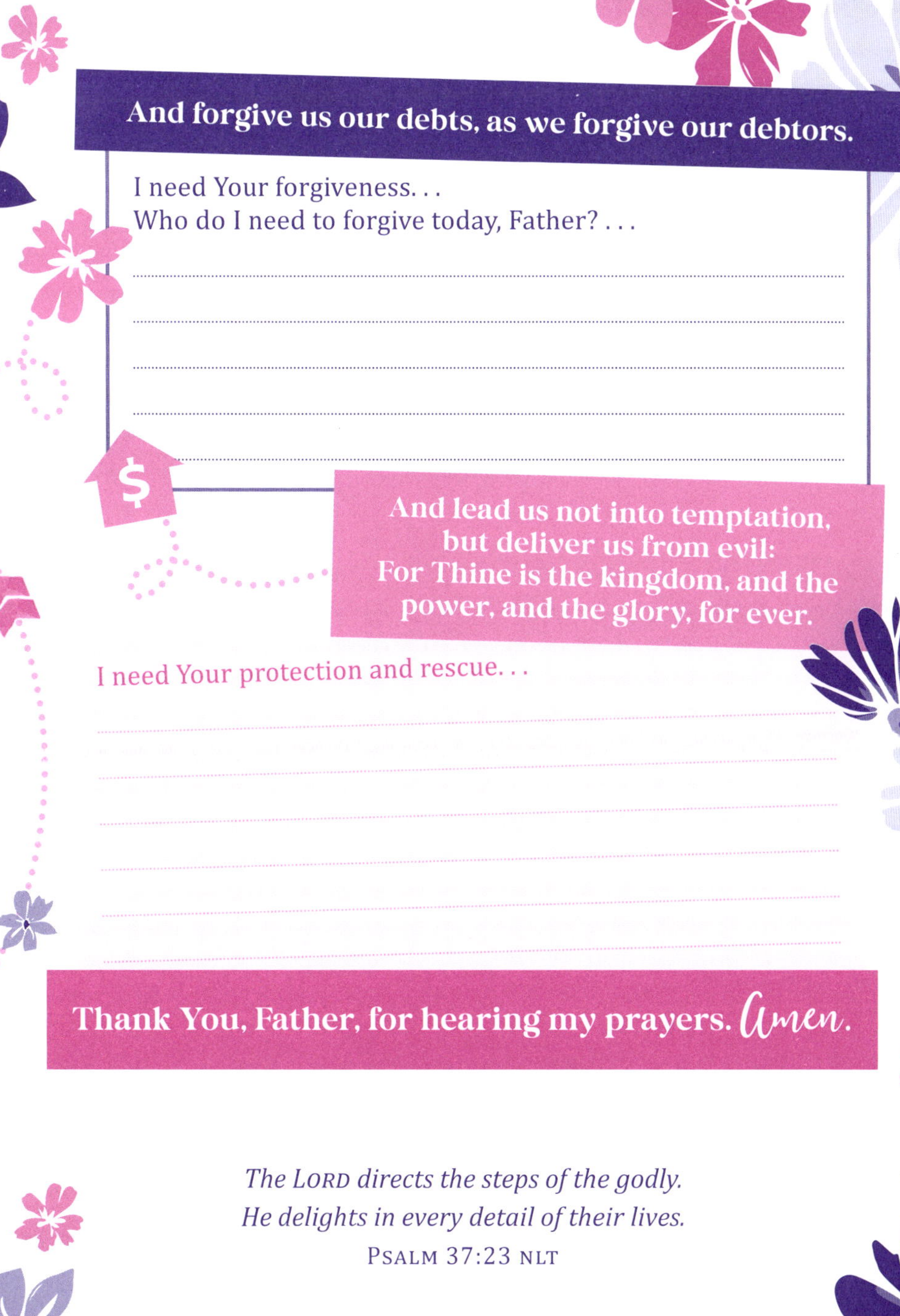

And forgive us our debts, as we forgive our debtors.

I need Your forgiveness. . .
Who do I need to forgive today, Father? . . .

**And lead us not into temptation,
but deliver us from evil:
For Thine is the kingdom, and the
power, and the glory, for ever.**

I need Your protection and rescue. . .

Thank You, Father, for hearing my prayers. Amen.

The LORD *directs the steps of the godly.*
He delights in every detail of their lives.
PSALM 37:23 NLT

Date:

Our Father which art in heaven, Hallowed be Thy name.

God, I want my life to honor You.
You have shown me Your favor in so many ways, including. . .

Thy kingdom come, Thy will be done in earth, as it is in heaven.

Please reveal Your good plans for my life.
I need Your guidance in these areas. . .

Give us this day our daily bread.

Thank You for providing for me.
Today, I am thankful for. . .

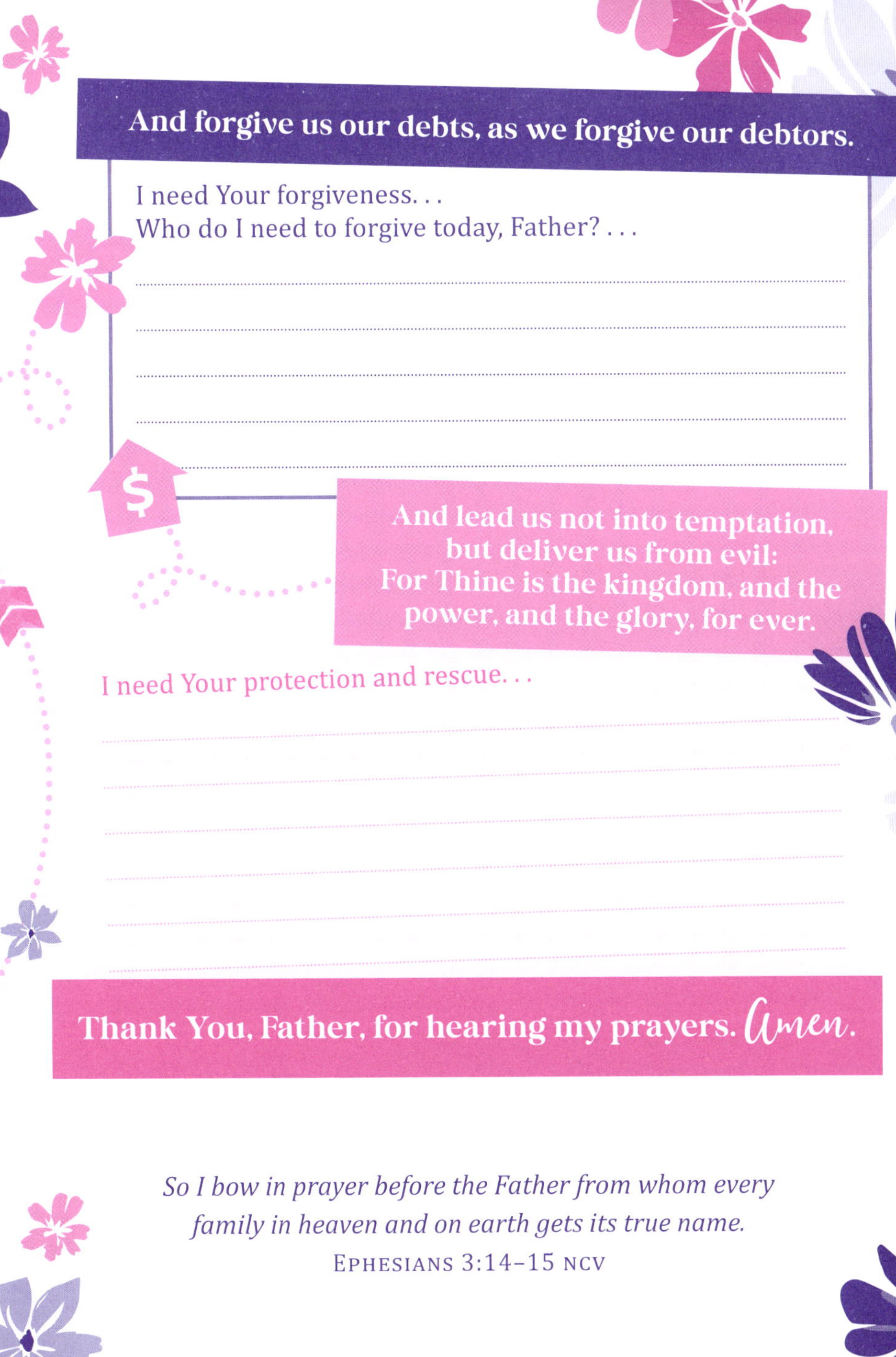

And forgive us our debts, as we forgive our debtors.

I need Your forgiveness. . .
Who do I need to forgive today, Father? . . .

And lead us not into temptation, but deliver us from evil: For Thine is the kingdom, and the power, and the glory, for ever.

I need Your protection and rescue. . .

Thank You, Father, for hearing my prayers. Amen.

So I bow in prayer before the Father from whom every family in heaven and on earth gets its true name.
EPHESIANS 3:14–15 NCV

Date:

Our Father which art in heaven, Hallowed be Thy name.

God, I want my life to honor You.
You have shown me Your favor in so many ways, including. . .

Thy kingdom come, Thy will be done in earth, as it is in heaven.

Please reveal Your good plans for my life.
I need Your guidance in these areas. . .

Give us this day our daily bread.

Thank You for providing for me.
Today, I am thankful for. . .

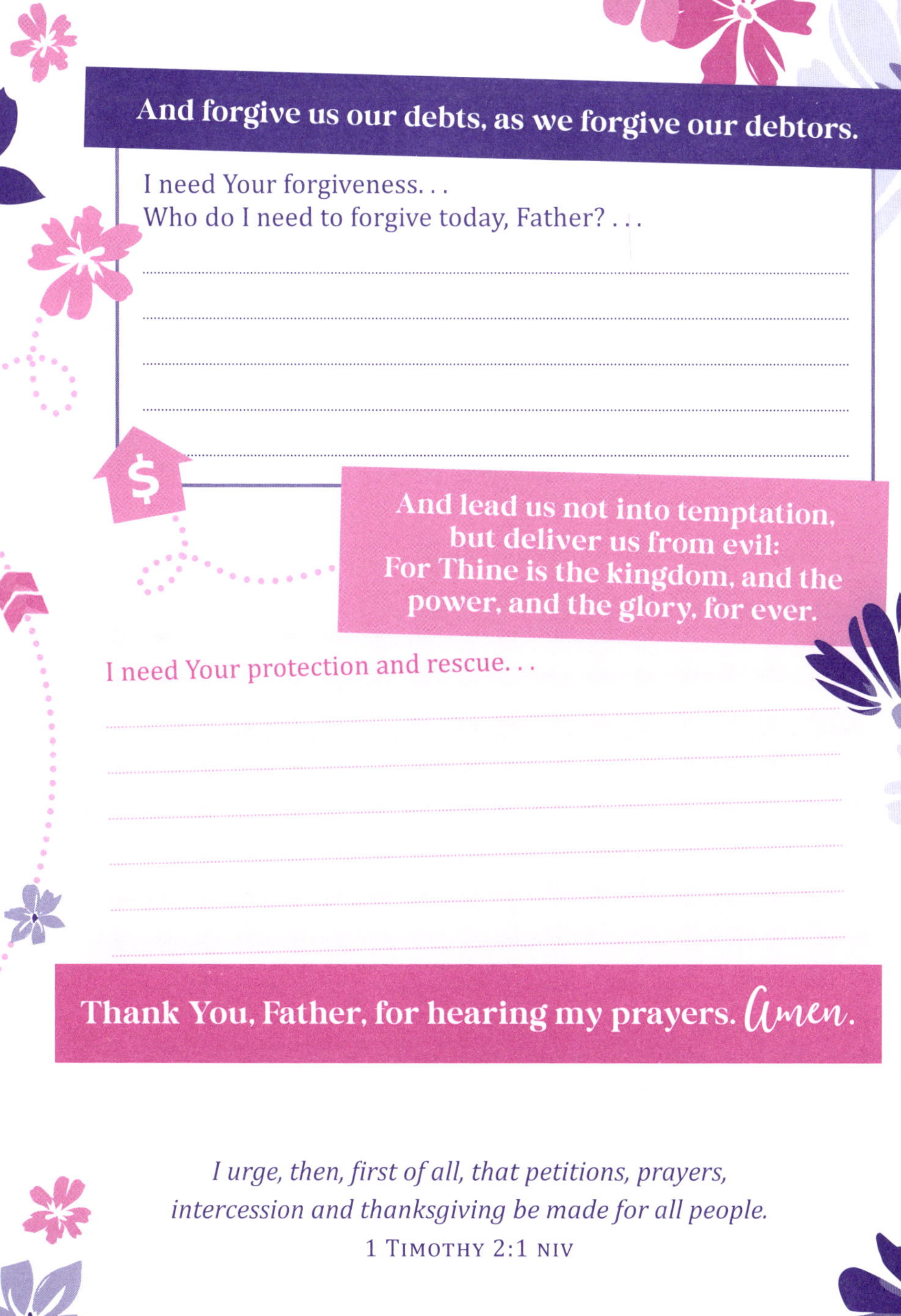

And forgive us our debts, as we forgive our debtors.

I need Your forgiveness. . .
Who do I need to forgive today, Father? . . .

And lead us not into temptation, but deliver us from evil: For Thine is the kingdom, and the power, and the glory, for ever.

I need Your protection and rescue. . .

Thank You, Father, for hearing my prayers. Amen.

I urge, then, first of all, that petitions, prayers, intercession and thanksgiving be made for all people.
1 Timothy 2:1 niv

Date:

Our Father which art in heaven, Hallowed be Thy name.

God, I want my life to honor You.
You have shown me Your favor in so many ways, including. . .

Thy kingdom come, Thy will be done in earth, as it is in heaven.

Please reveal Your good plans for my life.
I need Your guidance in these areas. . .

Give us this day our daily bread.

Thank You for providing for me.
Today, I am thankful for. . .

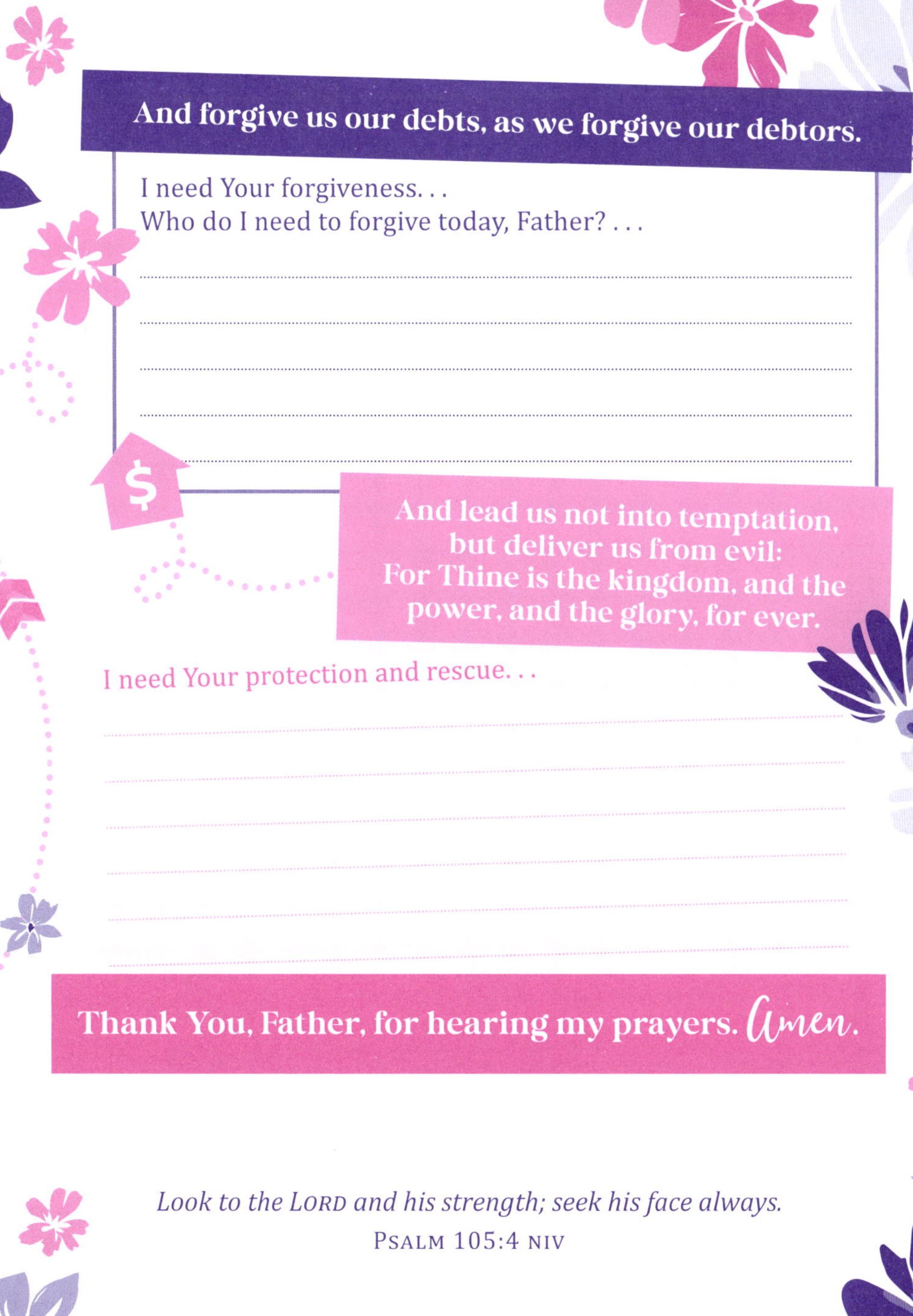

And forgive us our debts, as we forgive our debtors.

I need Your forgiveness. . .
Who do I need to forgive today, Father? . . .

And lead us not into temptation, but deliver us from evil: For Thine is the kingdom, and the power, and the glory, for ever.

I need Your protection and rescue. . .

Thank You, Father, for hearing my prayers. *Amen*.

Look to the Lord and his strength; seek his face always.
Psalm 105:4 NIV

Date:

Our Father which art in heaven, Hallowed be Thy name.

God, I want my life to honor You.
You have shown me Your favor in so many ways, including. . .

Thy kingdom come, Thy will be done in earth, as it is in heaven.

Please reveal Your good plans for my life.
I need Your guidance in these areas. . .

Give us this day our daily bread.

Thank You for providing for me.
Today, I am thankful for. . .

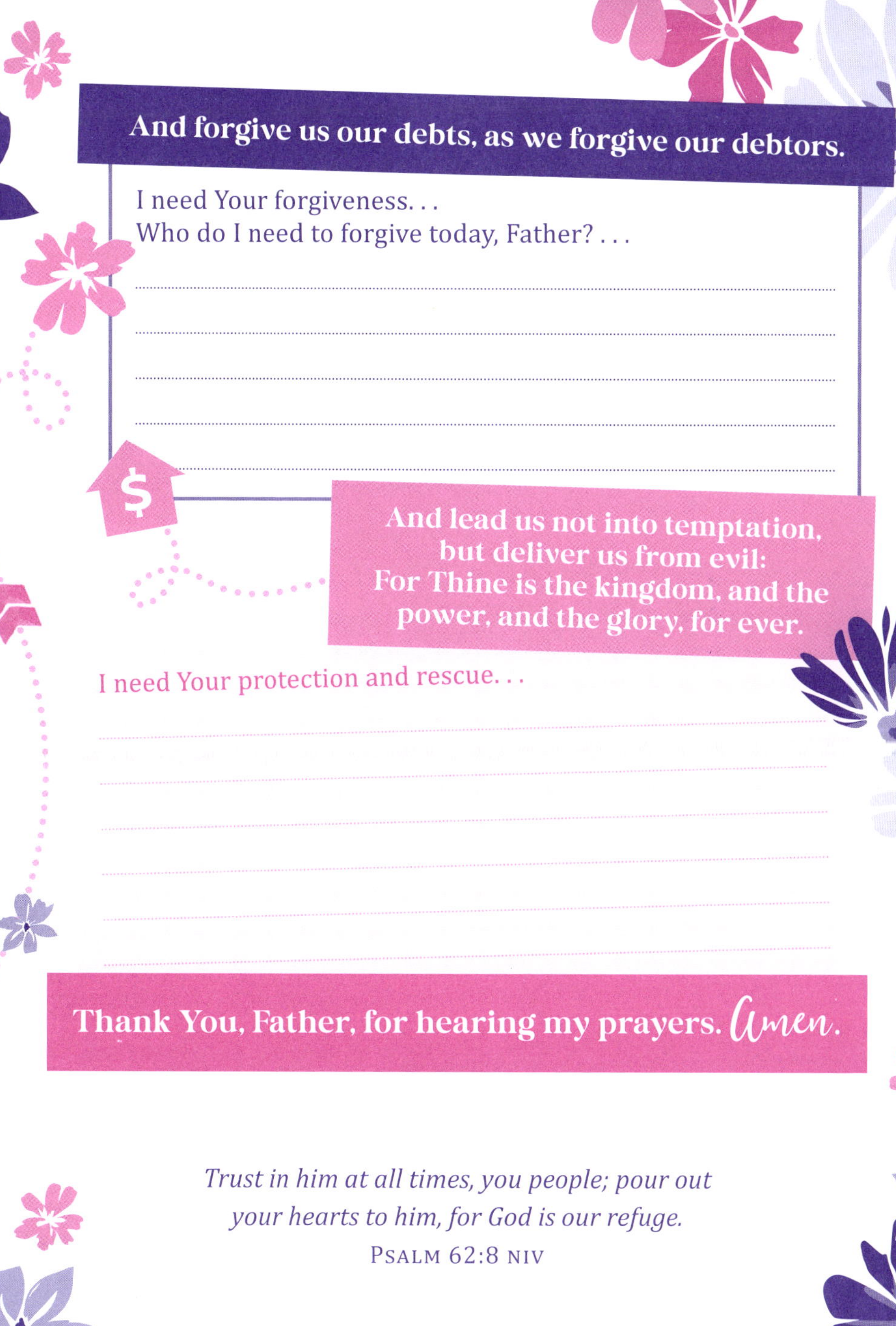

And forgive us our debts, as we forgive our debtors.

I need Your forgiveness. . .
Who do I need to forgive today, Father? . . .

And lead us not into temptation, but deliver us from evil: For Thine is the kingdom, and the power, and the glory, for ever.

I need Your protection and rescue. . .

Thank You, Father, for hearing my prayers. *Amen.*

Trust in him at all times, you people; pour out your hearts to him, for God is our refuge.
PSALM 62:8 NIV

Date:

Our Father which art in heaven, Hallowed be Thy name.

God, I want my life to honor You.
You have shown me Your favor in so many ways, including. . .

Thy kingdom come, Thy will be done in earth, as it is in heaven.

Please reveal Your good plans for my life.
I need Your guidance in these areas. . .

Give us this day our daily bread.

Thank You for providing for me.
Today, I am thankful for. . .

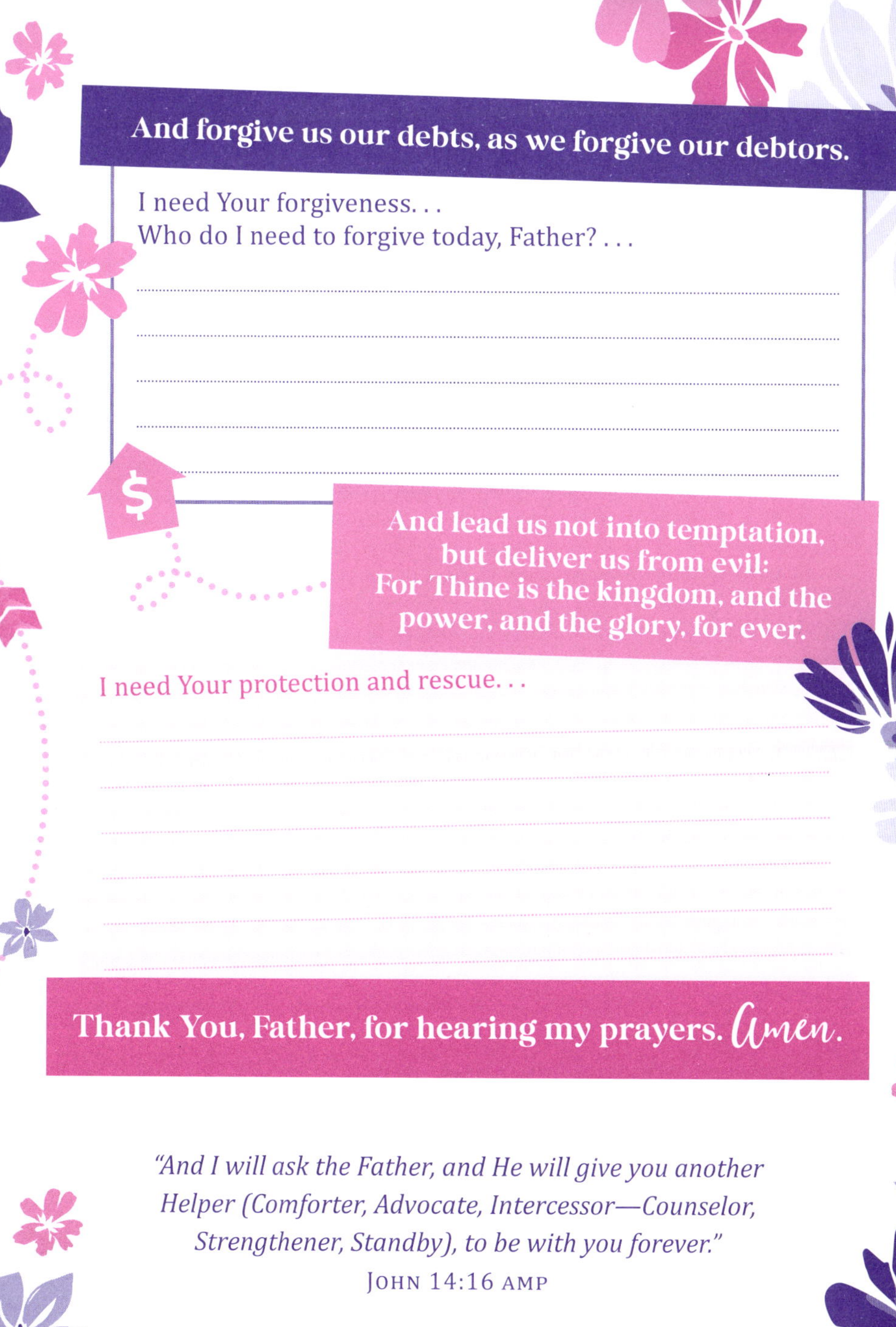

And forgive us our debts, as we forgive our debtors.

I need Your forgiveness. . .
Who do I need to forgive today, Father? . . .

And lead us not into temptation, but deliver us from evil: For Thine is the kingdom, and the power, and the glory, for ever.

I need Your protection and rescue. . .

Thank You, Father, for hearing my prayers. *Amen.*

"And I will ask the Father, and He will give you another Helper (Comforter, Advocate, Intercessor—Counselor, Strengthener, Standby), to be with you forever."
John 14:16 AMP

Date:

Our Father which art in heaven, Hallowed be Thy name.

God, I want my life to honor You.
You have shown me Your favor in so many ways, including. . .

Thy kingdom come, Thy will be done in earth, as it is in heaven.

Please reveal Your good plans for my life.
I need Your guidance in these areas. . .

Give us this day our daily bread.

Thank You for providing for me.
Today, I am thankful for. . .

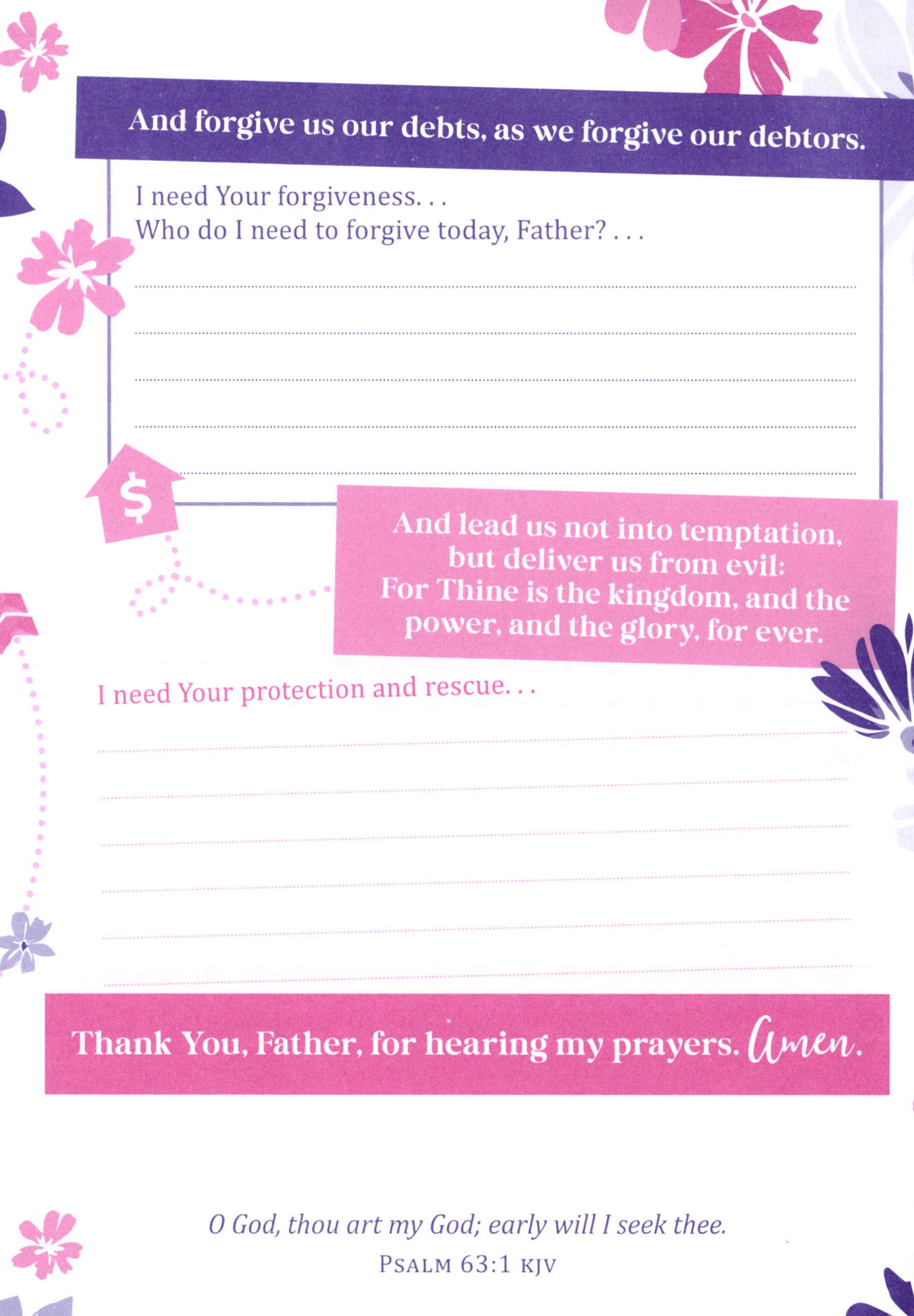

And forgive us our debts, as we forgive our debtors.

I need Your forgiveness. . .
Who do I need to forgive today, Father? . . .

And lead us not into temptation, but deliver us from evil: For Thine is the kingdom, and the power, and the glory, for ever.

I need Your protection and rescue. . .

Thank You, Father, for hearing my prayers. Amen.

O God, thou art my God; early will I seek thee.
Psalm 63:1 KJV

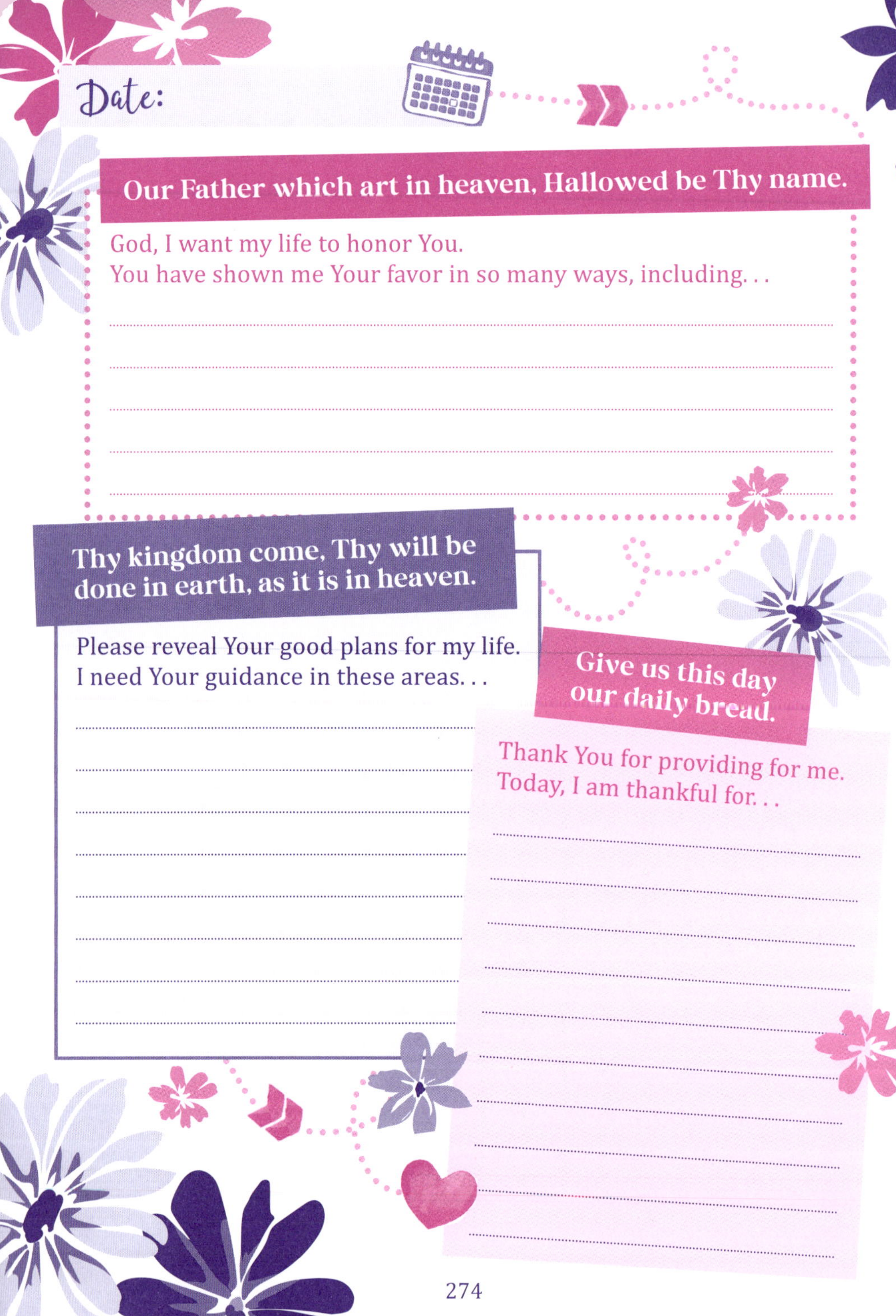

Date:

Our Father which art in heaven, Hallowed be Thy name.

God, I want my life to honor You.
You have shown me Your favor in so many ways, including. . .

Thy kingdom come, Thy will be done in earth, as it is in heaven.

Please reveal Your good plans for my life.
I need Your guidance in these areas. . .

Give us this day our daily bread.

Thank You for providing for me.
Today, I am thankful for. . .

And forgive us our debts, as we forgive our debtors.

I need Your forgiveness. . .
Who do I need to forgive today, Father? . . .

And lead us not into temptation, but deliver us from evil: For Thine is the kingdom, and the power, and the glory, for ever.

I need Your protection and rescue. . .

Thank You, Father, for hearing my prayers. Amen.

The Spirit of God, who raised Jesus from the dead, lives in you.
Romans 8:11 NLT

Section 6: When You Need Hope and Healing

AMNON AND TAMAR

And Tamar lived in her brother Absalom's house, a desolate woman.
2 Samuel 13:20 niv

Second Samuel 13 tells the tragic story of Amnon and Tamar. Amnon, one of King David's sons, raped his half sister, Tamar. Verse 18 says that Tamar dressed appropriately as a virgin daughter of the king. But after she was raped, Tamar exchanged her beautiful robe for the ashes of mourning.

Absalom, Tamar's full brother, was kind to her and took her into his home. Although she lived with him, scripture says that Absalom never said a word about her pain. The last time we read of Tamar is in 2 Samuel 13:20, "And Tamar lived in her brother Absalom's house, a desolate woman." Unfortunately, because of the culture of the time, Tamar would no longer be considered marriageable. The stigma of rape would remain with her, and this one event would shape the rest of Tamar's life.

Many women today also have been victimized. After experiencing pain and victimization, they, like Tamar, live desolate lives, allowing the experience to define them and determine their future. This does not have to be. Unlike Tamar, women today have choices.

No matter how dark your circumstances, God can redeem them. He can weave your pain into the tapestry of your life and provide hope, help, and healing. You can begin by speaking of the pain, then refusing to carry it. Open your heart to God today and receive the gift of healing.

Father, thank You for offering me hope and healing. Help me to let go of the pain of my past so that it does not define me. Redeem it for Your glory. Amen.

Date:

Dear Heavenly Father,

Today, I am feeling troubled about. . .

I need Your hope. . .

Please bring healing to. . .

My soul needs Your comforting touch in these areas. . .

I am thankful for. . .

Other things that I need to share with You, God. . .

Thank You, Father, for hearing my prayers. *Amen.*

The righteous cry out, and the LORD hears them;
he delivers them from all their troubles.
PSALM 34:17 NIV

Date:

Dear Heavenly Father,

Today, I am feeling troubled about. . .

I need Your hope. . .

Please bring healing to. . .

My soul needs Your comforting touch in these areas. . .

I am thankful for. . .

Other things that I need to share with You, God. . .

Thank You, Father, for hearing my prayers. Amen.

May integrity and uprightness protect me,
because my hope, Lord, is in you.
Psalm 25:21 NIV

Date:

Dear Heavenly Father,

Today, I am feeling troubled about. . .

I need Your hope. . .

Please bring healing to. . .

My soul needs Your comforting touch in these areas. . .

I am thankful for. . .

Other things that I need to share with You, God. . .

Thank You, Father, for hearing my prayers. *Amen.*

"But for you who fear my name, the Sun of Righteousness will rise with healing in his wings."
MALACHI 4:2 NLT

Date:

Dear Heavenly Father,

Today, I am feeling troubled about. . .

I need Your hope. . .

Please bring healing to. . .

My soul needs Your comforting touch in these areas. . .

I am thankful for. . .

Other things that I need to share with You, God. . .

Thank You, Father, for hearing my prayers. Amen.

Fear the L*ORD* *and turn away from evil. Then you will have healing for your body and strength for your bones.*
PROVERBS 3:7–8 NLT

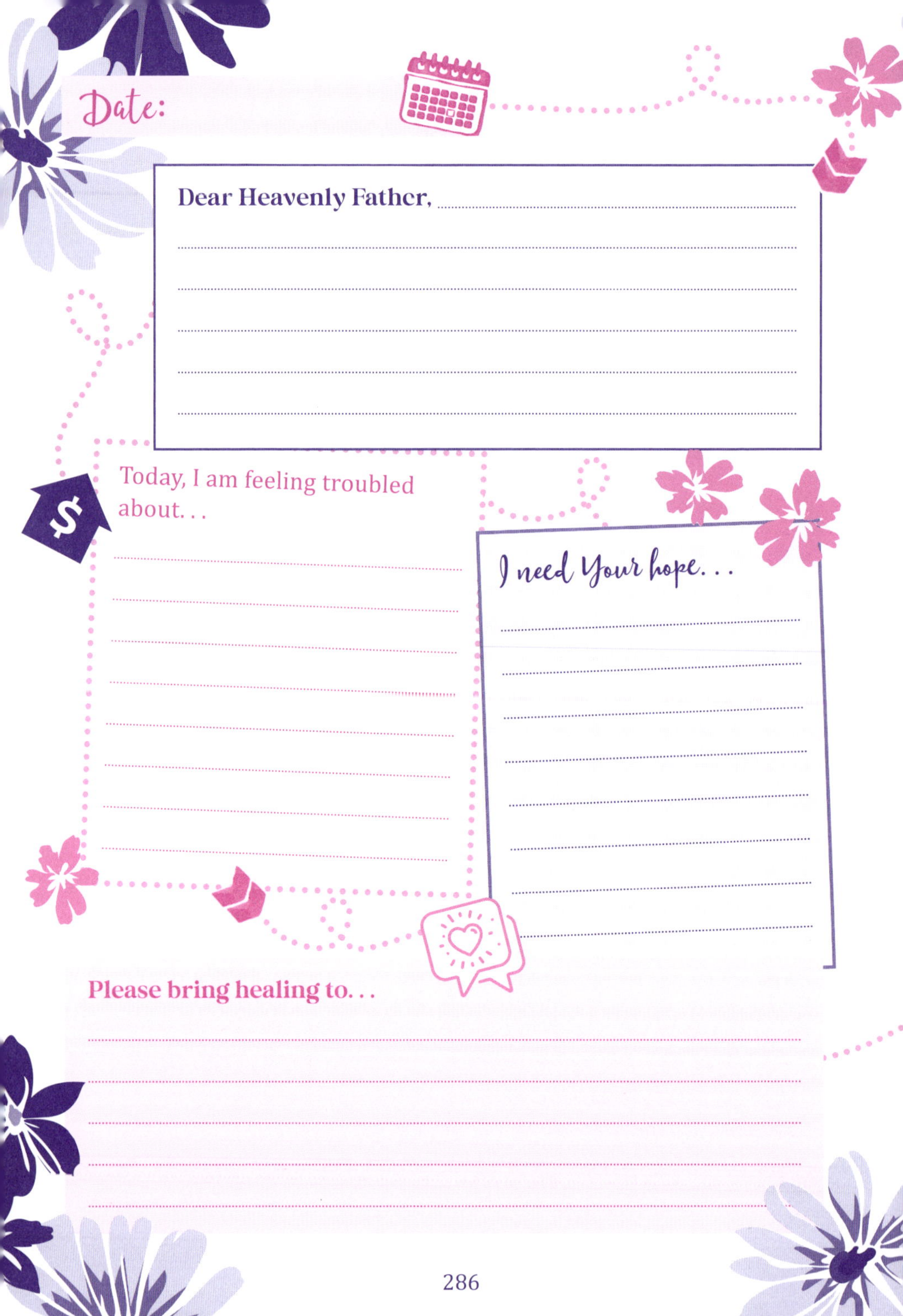

Date:

Dear Heavenly Father,

Today, I am feeling troubled about. . .

I need Your hope. . .

Please bring healing to. . .

My soul needs Your comforting touch in these areas. . .

I am thankful for. . .

Other things that I need to share with You, God. . .

Thank You, Father, for hearing my prayers. *Amen.*

May the God of hope fill you with all joy and peace in believing, so that by the power of the Holy Spirit you may abound in hope.
Romans 15:13 ESV

Date:

Dear Heavenly Father,

Today, I am feeling troubled about. . .

I need Your hope. . .

Please bring healing to. . .

My soul needs Your comforting touch in these areas. . .

I am thankful for. . .

Other things that I need to share with You, God. . .

Thank You, Father, for hearing my prayers. *Amen.*

Seek the Lord and his strength;
seek his presence continually!
Psalm 105:4 ESV

Date:

Dear Heavenly Father,

Today, I am feeling troubled about. . .

I need Your hope. . .

Please bring healing to. . .

My soul needs Your comforting touch in these areas. . .

I am thankful for. . .

Other things that I need to share with You, God. . .

Thank You, Father, for hearing my prayers. *Amen.*

But you, LORD, are a shield around me,
my glory, the One who lifts my head high.
PSALM 3:3 NIV

Date:

Dear Heavenly Father,

Today, I am feeling troubled about. . .

I need Your hope. . .

Please bring healing to. . .

My soul needs Your comforting touch in these areas. . .

I am thankful for. . .

Other things that I need to share with You, God. . .

Thank You, Father, for hearing my prayers. *Amen.*

Now, may the Lord himself, the Lord of
peace, pour into you his peace in every
circumstance and in every possible way.
The Lord's tangible presence be with you all.
2 Thessalonians 3:16 TPT

Date:

Dear Heavenly Father,

Today, I am feeling troubled about. . .

I need Your hope. . .

Please bring healing to. . .

My soul needs Your comforting touch in these areas. . .

I am thankful for. . .

Other things that I need to share with You, God. . .

Thank You, Father, for hearing my prayers. *Amen.*

God, the one and only. . . . Everything I hope for comes from him. . . . He's solid rock under my feet, breathing room for my soul. . . : I'm set for life.

Psalm 62:5–6 msg

Date:

Dear Heavenly Father,

Today, I am feeling troubled about. . .

I need Your hope. . .

Please bring healing to. . .

My soul needs Your comforting touch in these areas. . .

I am thankful for. . .

Other things that I need to share with You, God. . .

Thank You, Father, for hearing my prayers. Amen.

Pray about everything. He longs to hear your requests, so talk to God about your needs and be thankful for what has come.

PHILIPPIANS 4:6 VOICE

Date:

Dear Heavenly Father,

Today, I am feeling troubled about...

I need Your hope...

Please bring healing to...

My soul needs Your comforting touch in these areas. . .

I am thankful for. . .

Other things that I need to share with You, God. . .

Thank You, Father, for hearing my prayers. *Amen.*

Those who walk the fields to sow, casting their seed in tears, will one day tread those same long rows, amazed by what's appeared.

Psalm 126:5 voice

Date:

Dear Heavenly Father,

Today, I am feeling troubled about. . .

I need Your hope. . .

Please bring healing to. . .

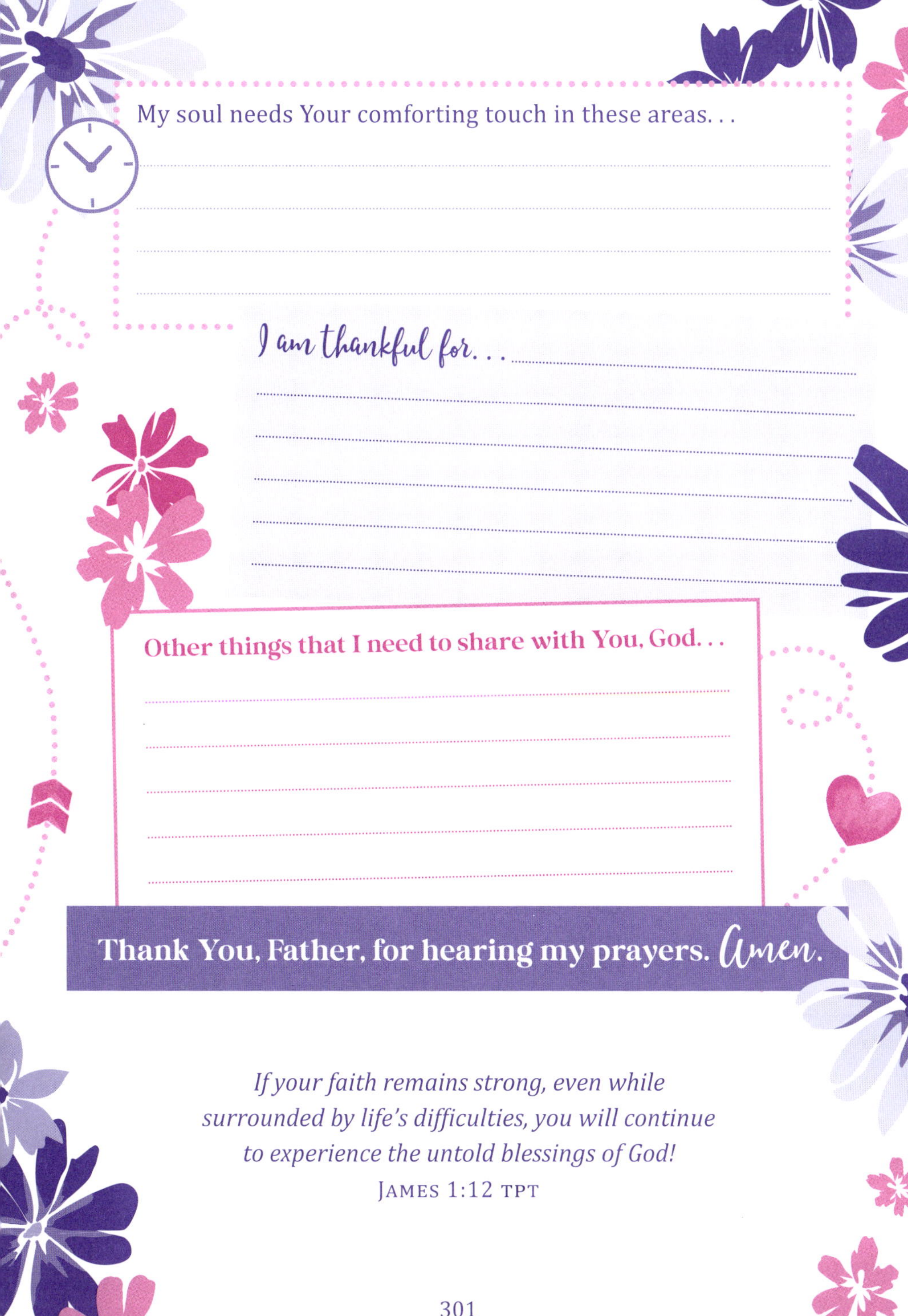

My soul needs Your comforting touch in these areas. . .

I am thankful for. . .

Other things that I need to share with You, God. . .

Thank You, Father, for hearing my prayers. Amen.

If your faith remains strong, even while surrounded by life's difficulties, you will continue to experience the untold blessings of God!

James 1:12 TPT

Date:

Dear Heavenly Father,

Today, I am feeling troubled about. . .

I need Your hope. . .

Please bring healing to. . .

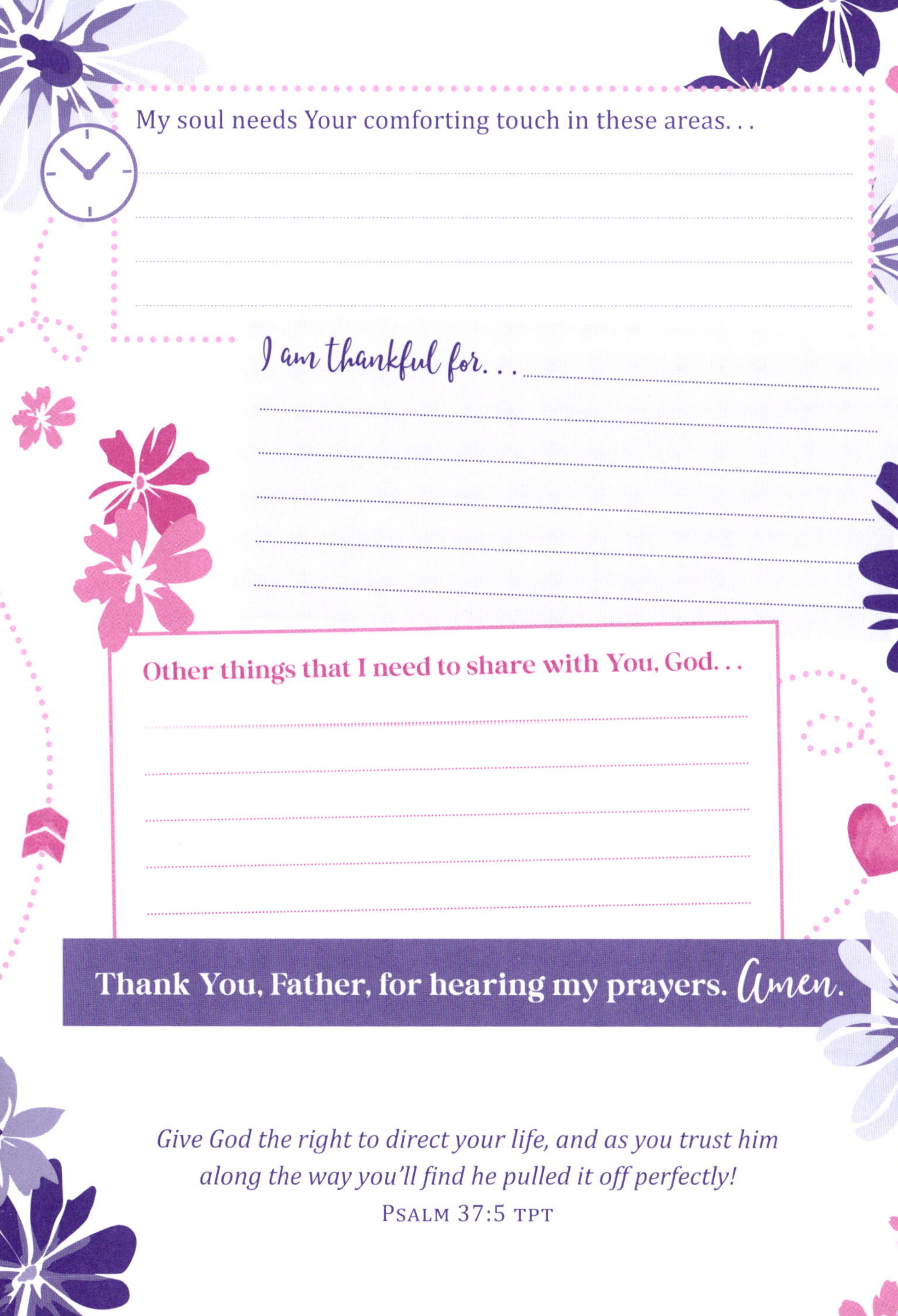

My soul needs Your comforting touch in these areas. . .

I am thankful for. . .

Other things that I need to share with You, God. . .

Thank You, Father, for hearing my prayers. Amen.

Give God the right to direct your life, and as you trust him along the way you'll find he pulled it off perfectly!

PSALM 37:5 TPT

Date:

Dear Heavenly Father,

Today, I am feeling troubled about. . .

I need Your hope. . .

Please bring healing to. . .

My soul needs Your comforting touch in these areas. . .

I am thankful for. . .

Other things that I need to share with You, God. . .

Thank You, Father, for hearing my prayers. Amen.

So now you need to rethink everything and turn to God so your sins will be forgiven and a new day can dawn, days of refreshing times flowing from the Lord.

Acts 3:19 voice

Date:

Dear Heavenly Father,

Today, I am feeling troubled about. . .

I need Your hope. . .

Please bring healing to. . .

My soul needs Your comforting touch in these areas. . .

I am thankful for. . .

Other things that I need to share with You, God. . .

Thank You, Father, for hearing my prayers. Amen.

So I say to my soul, "Don't be discouraged. Don't be disturbed. For I know my God will break through for me." Then I'll have plenty of reasons to praise him all over again.

PSALM 42:11 TPT

Date:

Dear Heavenly Father,

Today, I am feeling troubled about. . .

I need Your hope. . .

Please bring healing to. . .

My soul needs Your comforting touch in these areas. . .

I am thankful for. . .

Other things that I need to share with You, God. . .

Thank You, Father, for hearing my prayers. *Amen.*

For when I was desperate, overwhelmed, and about to give up, you were the only one there to help. You gave me a way of escape from the hidden traps of my enemies.

Psalm 142:3 TPT

Date:

Dear Heavenly Father,

Today, I am feeling troubled about. . .

I need Your hope. . .

Please bring healing to. . .

My soul needs Your comforting touch in these areas. . .

I am thankful for. . .

Other things that I need to share with You, God. . .

Thank You, Father, for hearing my prayers. Amen.

Let your unfailing love surround us, LORD,
for our hope is in you alone.
PSALM 33:22 NLT

Date:

Dear Heavenly Father,

Today, I am feeling troubled about. . .

I need Your hope. . .

Please bring healing to. . .

My soul needs Your comforting touch in these areas. . .

I am thankful for. . .

Other things that I need to share with You, God. . .

Thank You, Father, for hearing my prayers. Amen.

And [Jesus] said. . . , "Daughter, your faith has made you well; go in peace and be cured of your disease."

Mark 5:34 NASB

Date:

Dear Heavenly Father,

Today, I am feeling troubled about. . .

I need Your hope. . .

Please bring healing to. . .

My soul needs Your comforting touch in these areas. . .

I am thankful for. . .

Other things that I need to share with You, God. . .

Thank You, Father, for hearing my prayers. *Amen.*

Guide me in your truth and teach me, for you are God my Savior, and my hope is in you all day long.

Psalm 25:5 NIV

Date:

Dear Heavenly Father,

Today, I am feeling troubled about. . .

I need Your hope. . .

Please bring healing to. . .

My soul needs Your comforting touch in these areas. . .

I am thankful for. . .

Other things that I need to share with You, God. . .

Thank You, Father, for hearing my prayers. *Amen.*

I love the Lord *because he hears my voice and my prayer for mercy. Because he bends down to listen, I will pray as long as I have breath!*

Psalm 116:1–2 NLT

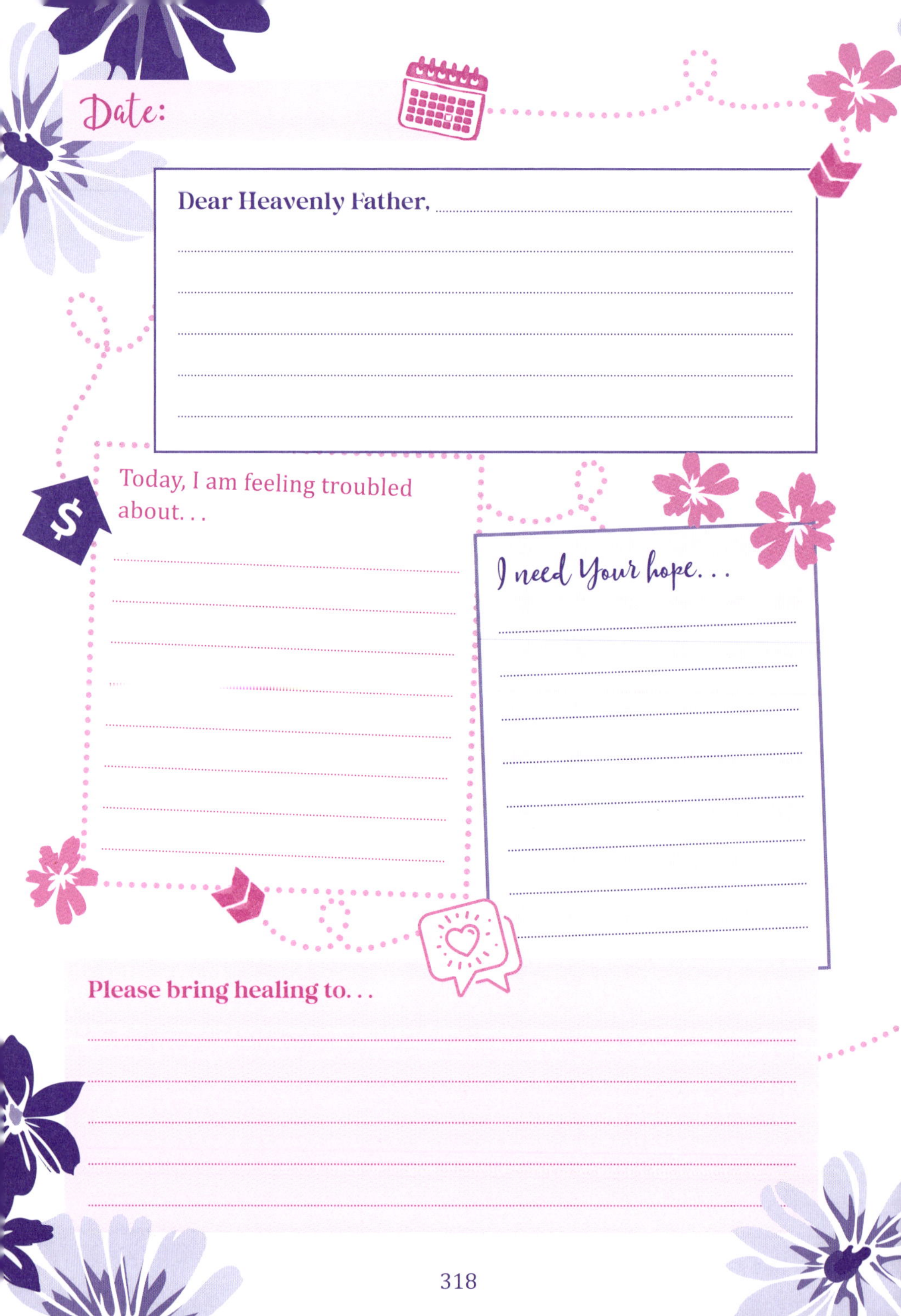

Date:

Dear Heavenly Father,

Today, I am feeling troubled about. . .

I need Your hope. . .

Please bring healing to. . .

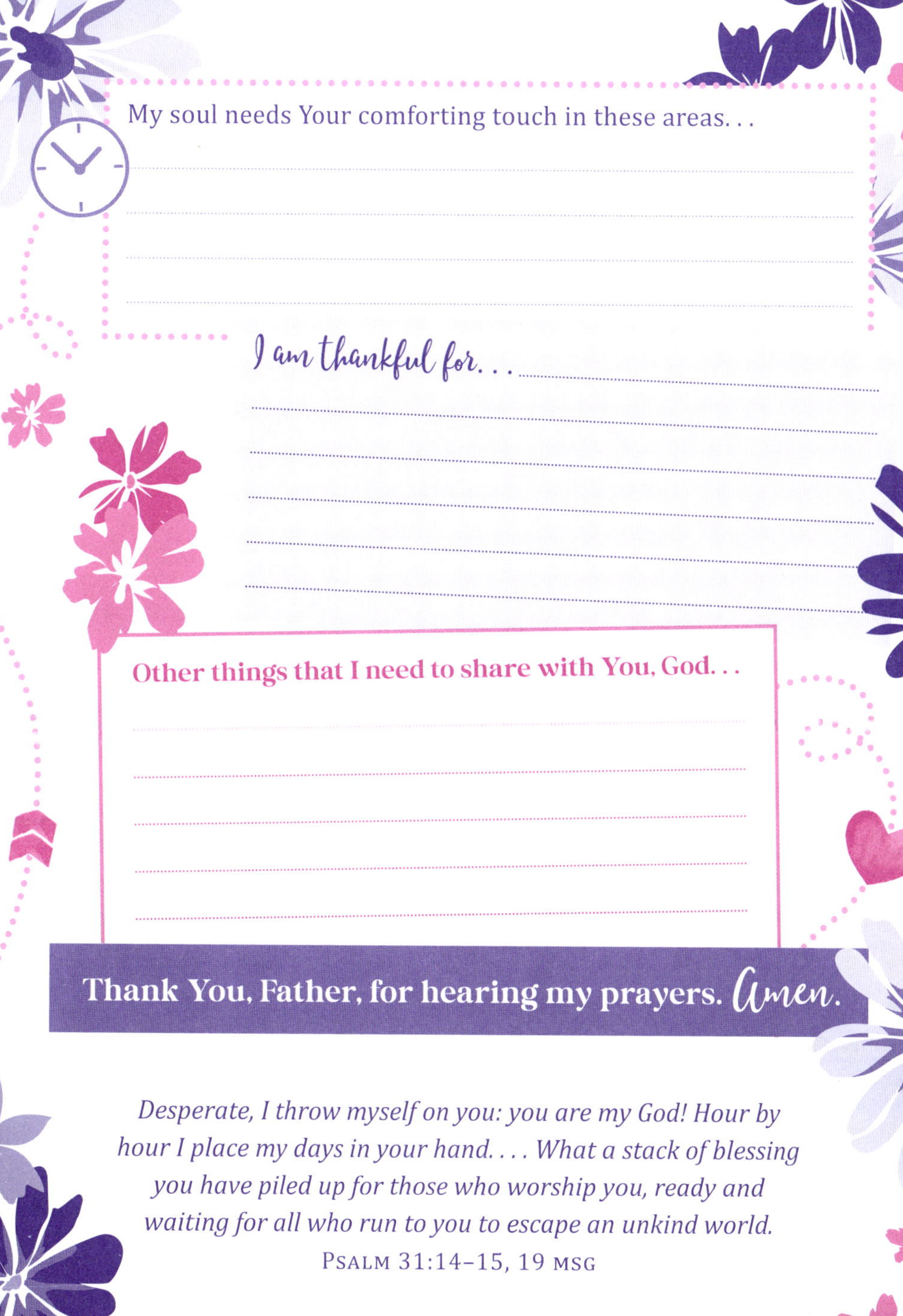

My soul needs Your comforting touch in these areas. . .

I am thankful for. . .

Other things that I need to share with You, God. . .

Thank You, Father, for hearing my prayers. *Amen.*

Desperate, I throw myself on you: you are my God! Hour by hour I place my days in your hand. . . . What a stack of blessing you have piled up for those who worship you, ready and waiting for all who run to you to escape an unkind world.

Psalm 31:14–15, 19 msg

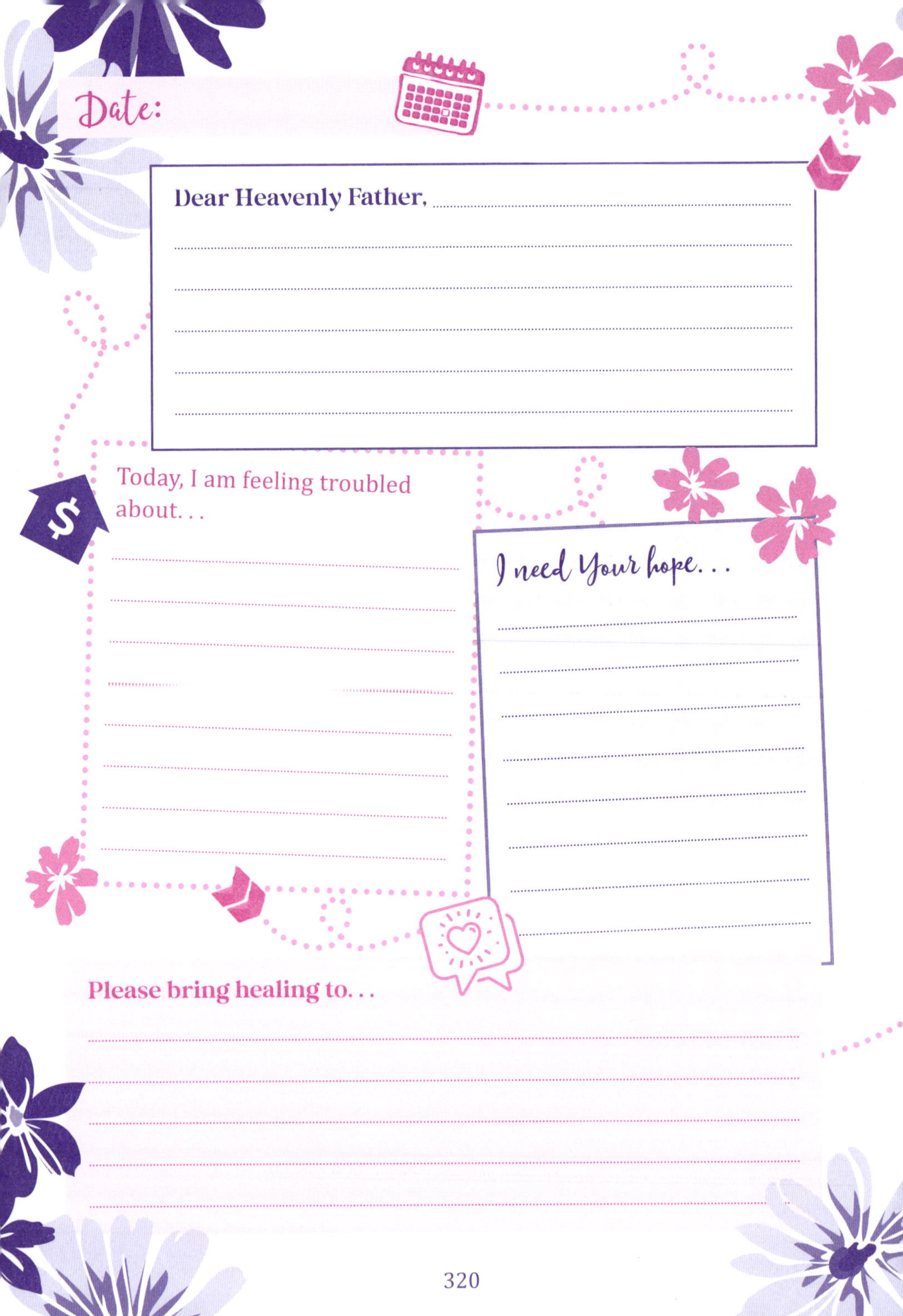

Date:

Dear Heavenly Father,

Today, I am feeling troubled about. . .

I need Your hope. . .

Please bring healing to. . .

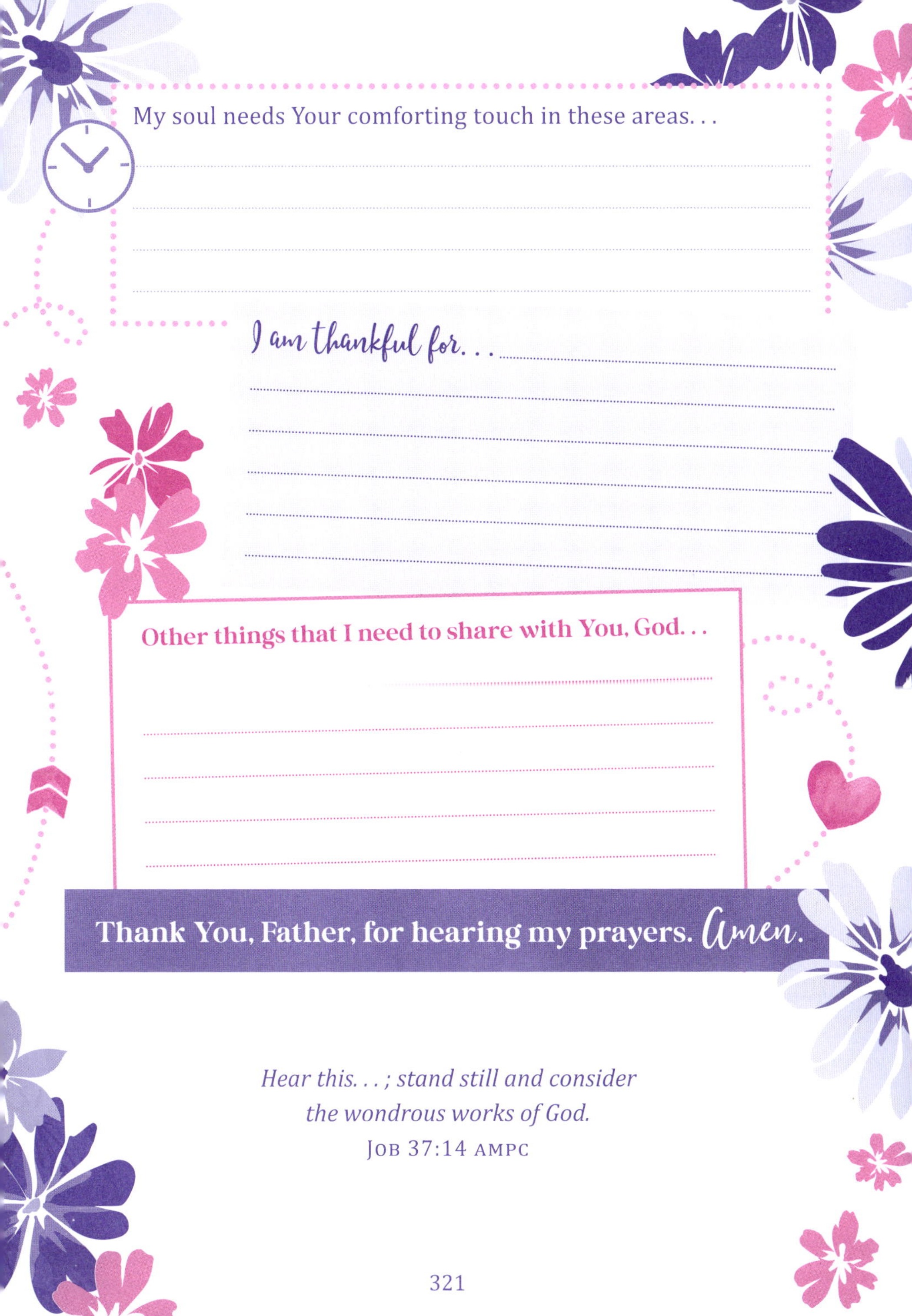

My soul needs Your comforting touch in these areas. . .

I am thankful for. . .

Other things that I need to share with You, God. . .

Thank You, Father, for hearing my prayers. Amen.

Hear this. . . ; stand still and consider the wondrous works of God.
Job 37:14 AMPC

Date:

Dear Heavenly Father,

Today, I am feeling troubled about. . .

I need Your hope. . .

Please bring healing to. . .

My soul needs Your comforting touch in these areas. . .

I am thankful for. . .

Other things that I need to share with You, God. . .

Thank You, Father, for hearing my prayers. *Amen.*

Likewise the Spirit helps us in our weakness. For we do not know what to pray for as we ought, but the Spirit himself intercedes for us with groanings too deep for words.

Romans 8:26 ESV

Date:

Dear Heavenly Father,

Today, I am feeling troubled about. . .

I need Your hope. . .

Please bring healing to. . .

My soul needs Your comforting touch in these areas. . .

I am thankful for. . .

Other things that I need to share with You, God. . .

Thank You, Father, for hearing my prayers. Amen.

If you don't know what you're doing, pray to the Father. He loves to help. You'll get his help, and won't be condescended to when you ask for it. Ask boldly, believingly, without a second thought.
JAMES 1:5–6 MSG

Date:

Dear Heavenly Father,

Today, I am feeling troubled about. . .

I need Your hope. . .

Please bring healing to. . .

My soul needs Your comforting touch in these areas. . .

I am thankful for. . .

Other things that I need to share with You, God. . .

Thank You, Father, for hearing my prayers. Amen.

The hopes of the godly result in happiness.
PROVERBS 10:28 NLT

Section 7:

When You Want a Good Start to Your Morning

WEARY DAYS

Why art thou cast down, O my soul? and why art thou disquieted in me? hope thou in God: for I shall yet praise him for the help of his countenance. O my God, my soul is cast down within me: therefore will I remember thee from the land of Jordan, and of the Hermonites, from the hill Mizar.

Psalm 42:5–6 kjv

It's easy for life's responsibilities and commitments to drag us down. Each day seems like a repeat of the day before. The morning alarm becomes our enemy, and the snooze button becomes our considerate companion. Our hard work often goes unappreciated. Nothing feels accomplished. Our soul yearns for something more.

If we accept it, God's constant goodness can be our delight. In the mornings, instead of our groaning and hiding beneath the pillows, God desires for us to communicate with Him. His voice could be the first one that we hear each day. As we roll over and stretch, we can then say, "I love You, God. Thank You for another day of life."

Our willingness to speak with God at the day's beginning shows our dependence on Him. We can't make it alone. It is a comforting truth that God never intended for us to trek through the hours unaccompanied. He promises to be with us. He also promises His guidance and direction as we meet people and receive opportunities to serve Him.

Getting started is as simple as removing our head from beneath the pillows and telling God good morning.

Lord, refresh my spirit and give me joy for today's activities. Amen.

Date:

Good morning, God!

I'm feeling. . .

As I begin my day, I want to share. . .

Please infuse my heart with Your joy!

Help me to accomplish. . .

I am fully giving these worries and concerns to You. . .

Thank You for. . .

Other things I need to share with You, God. . .

Thank You, Father, for hearing my prayers. *Amen.*

The faithful love of the Lord *never ends!*
His mercies never cease. Great is his faithfulness;
his mercies begin afresh each morning.
Lamentations 3:22–23 NLT

Date:

Good morning, God!

As I begin my day, I want to share. . .

I'm feeling. . .

Please infuse my heart with Your joy!

Help me to accomplish. . .

I am fully giving these worries and concerns to You. . .

Thank You for. . .

Other things I need to share with You, God. . .

Thank You, Father, for hearing my prayers. Amen.

In the morning you will see the glory of the LORD.
EXODUS 16:7 NLT

Date:

Good morning, God!

As I begin my day, I want to share. . .

I'm feeling. . .

Please infuse my heart with Your joy!

Help me to accomplish. . .

I am fully giving these worries and concerns to You. . .

Thank You for. . .

Other things I need to share with You, God. . .

Thank You, Father, for hearing my prayers. *Amen.*

The LORD is my shepherd, I lack nothing.
He makes me lie down in green pastures, he leads
me beside quiet waters, he refreshes my soul.
PSALM 23:1–3 NIV

Date:

Good morning, God!

I'm feeling. . .

As I begin my day, I want to share. . .

Please infuse my heart with Your joy!

Help me to accomplish. . .

I am fully giving these worries and concerns to You. . .

Thank You for. . .

Other things I need to share with You, God. . .

Thank You, Father, for hearing my prayers. *Amen.*

I wait for the Lord more than
watchmen wait for the morning.
Psalm 130:6 niv

Date:

Good morning, God!

As I begin my day, I want to share. . .

I'm feeling. . .

Please infuse my heart with Your joy!

Help me to accomplish. . .

I am fully giving these worries and concerns to You. . .

Thank You for. . .

Other things I need to share with You, God. . .

Thank You, Father, for hearing my prayers. *Amen.*

Put God in charge of your work,
then what you've planned will take place.
Proverbs 16:3 MSG

Date:

Good morning, God!

As I begin my day, I want to share. . .

I'm feeling. . .

Please infuse my heart with Your joy!

Help me to accomplish. . .

I am fully giving these worries and concerns to You. . .

Thank You for. . .

Other things I need to share with You, God. . .

Thank You, Father, for hearing my prayers. *Amen.*

This is the day the Lord *has made.*
We will rejoice and be glad in it.
Psalm 118:24 NLT

Date:

Good morning, God!

I'm feeling. . .

Please infuse my heart with Your joy!

As I begin my day, I want to share. . .

Help me to accomplish. . .

I am fully giving these worries and concerns to You...

Thank You for...

Other things I need to share with You, God...

Thank You, Father, for hearing my prayers. *Amen.*

It is good to proclaim your unfailing love in the morning, your faithfulness in the evening.
PSALM 92:2 NLT

Date:
Good morning, God!
As I begin my day, I want to share. . .
I'm feeling. . .
Please infuse my heart with Your joy!
Help me to accomplish. . .

I am fully giving these worries and concerns to You. . .

Thank You for. . .

Other things I need to share with You, God. . .

Thank You, Father, for hearing my prayers. *Amen.*

Let me hear of your unfailing love each morning, for I am trusting you. Show me where to walk, for I give myself to you.

PSALM 143:8 NLT

Date:

Good morning, God!

As I begin my day, I want to share. . .

I'm feeling. . .

Please infuse my heart with Your joy!

Help me to accomplish. . .

I am fully giving these worries and concerns to You. . .

Thank You for. . .

Other things I need to share with You, God. . .

Thank You, Father, for hearing my prayers. *Amen.*

For he will command his angels concerning you to guard you in all your ways.

Psalm 91:11 NIV

Date:

Good morning, God!

As I begin my day, I want to share. . .

I'm feeling. . .

Please infuse my heart with Your joy!

Help me to accomplish. . .

I am fully giving these worries and concerns to You. . .

Thank You for. . .

Other things I need to share with You, God. . .

Thank You, Father, for hearing my prayers. *Amen.*

Morning, noon, and night. . .the Lord hears my voice.
Psalm 55:17 NLT

Date:

Good morning, God!

I'm feeling. . .

As I begin my day, I want to share. . .

Please infuse my heart with Your joy!

Help me to accomplish. . .

I am fully giving these worries and concerns to You. . .

Thank You for. . .

Other things I need to share with You, God. . .

Thank You, Father, for hearing my prayers. *Amen.*

Stay wide-awake in prayer. Most of all,
love each other as if your life depended on it.
Love makes up for practically anything.
1 Peter 4:7–8 MSG

Date:

Good morning, God!

As I begin my day, I want to share. . .

I'm feeling. . .

Please infuse my heart with Your joy!

Help me to accomplish. . .

I am fully giving these worries and concerns to You. . .

Thank You for. . .

Other things I need to share with You, God. . .

Thank You, Father, for hearing my prayers. *Amen.*

Blessed be God—he heard me praying. He proved he's on my side; I've thrown my lot in with him.

Psalm 28:6 MSG

Date:

Good morning, God!

As I begin my day, I want to share. . .

I'm feeling. . .

Please infuse my heart with Your joy!

Help me to accomplish. . .

I am fully giving these worries and concerns to You. . .

Thank You for. . .

Other things I need to share with You, God. . .

Thank You, Father, for hearing my prayers. *Amen.*

Listen to my voice in the morning, Lord. Each morning I bring my requests to you and wait expectantly.

Psalm 5:3 NLT

Date:

Good morning, God!

As I begin my day, I want to share. . .

I'm feeling. . .

Please infuse my heart with Your joy!

Help me to accomplish. . .

I am fully giving these worries and concerns to You. . .

Thank You for. . .

Other things I need to share with You, God. . .

Thank You, Father, for hearing my prayers. *Amen.*

Let every living, breathing creature praise GOD!

PSALM 150:6 MSG

Date:

Good morning, God!

As I begin my day, I want to share. . .

I'm feeling. . .

Please infuse my heart with Your joy!

Help me to accomplish. . .

I am fully giving these worries and concerns to You. . .

Thank You for. . .

Other things I need to share with You, God. . .

Thank You, Father, for hearing my prayers. *Amen.*

Because your love is better than life, my lips will glorify you. I will praise you as long as I live, and in your name I will lift up my hands.

Psalm 63:3–4 NIV

Date:

Good morning, God!

As I begin my day, I want to share. . .

I'm feeling. . .

Please infuse my heart with Your joy!

Help me to accomplish. . .

I am fully giving these worries and concerns to You. . .

Thank You for. . .

Other things I need to share with You, God. . .

Thank You, Father, for hearing my prayers. *Amen.*

Each morning I will sing with joy about your unfailing love. For you have been my refuge, a place of safety when I am in distress.

PSALM 59:16 NLT

Date:

Good morning, God!

As I begin my day, I want to share. . .

I'm feeling. . .

Please infuse my heart with Your joy!

Help me to accomplish. . .

I am fully giving these worries and concerns to You. . .

Thank You for. . .

Other things I need to share with You, God. . .

Thank You, Father, for hearing my prayers. Amen.

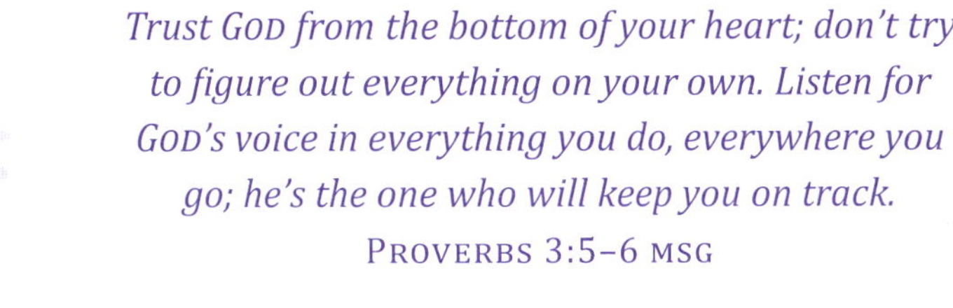

Trust God from the bottom of your heart; don't try to figure out everything on your own. Listen for God's voice in everything you do, everywhere you go; he's the one who will keep you on track.

Proverbs 3:5–6 MSG

Date:

Good morning, God!

As I begin my day, I want to share. . .

I'm feeling. . .

Please infuse my heart with Your joy!

Help me to accomplish. . .

I am fully giving these worries and concerns to You. . .

Thank You for. . .

Other things I need to share with You, God. . .

Thank You, Father, for hearing my prayers. *Amen.*

O Lord, I cry out to you. I will keep on pleading day by day.

Psalm 88:13 NLT

Date:

Good morning, God!

As I begin my day, I want to share. . .

I'm feeling. . .

Please infuse my heart with Your joy!

Help me to accomplish. . .

I am fully giving these worries and concerns to You. . .

Thank You for. . .

Other things I need to share with You, God. . .

Thank You, Father, for hearing my prayers. Amen.

God, make a fresh start in me.

Psalm 51:10 msg

Date:

Good morning, God!

As I begin my day, I want to share. . .

I'm feeling. . .

Please infuse my heart with Your joy!

Help me to accomplish. . .

I am fully giving these worries and concerns to You. . .

Thank You for. . .

Other things I need to share with You, God. . .

Thank You, Father, for hearing my prayers. Amen.

Weeping may last through the night,
but joy comes with the morning.
Psalm 30:5 NLT

Date:
Good morning, God!
As I begin my day, I want to share. . .
I'm feeling. . .
Please infuse my heart with Your joy!
Help me to accomplish. . .

I am fully giving these worries and concerns to You. . .

Thank You for. . .

Other things I need to share with You, God. . .

Thank You, Father, for hearing my prayers. Amen.

The wise counsel God *gives when I'm awake is confirmed by my sleeping heart. Day and night I'll stick with* God*; I've got a good thing going and I'm not letting go.*

Psalm 16:7–8 msg

Date:

Good morning, God!

As I begin my day, I want to share. . .

I'm feeling. . .

Please infuse my heart with Your joy!

Help me to accomplish. . .

I am fully giving these worries and concerns to You. . .

Thank You for. . .

Other things I need to share with You, God. . .

Thank You, Father, for hearing my prayers. Amen.

I'm ready, God, so ready, ready from head to toe, ready to sing, ready to raise a tune: "Wake up, soul! Wake up, harp! wake up, lute! Wake up, you sleepyhead sun!"

PSALM 57:7–8 MSG

Date:
Good morning, God!
As I begin my day, I want to share. . .
I'm feeling. . .
Please infuse my heart with Your joy!
Help me to accomplish. . .

I am fully giving these worries and concerns to You. . .

Thank You for. . .

Other things I need to share with You, God. . .

Thank You, Father, for hearing my prayers. Amen.

Hurry with your answer, God! . . . Don't turn away; don't ignore me! . . . If you wake me each morning with the sound of your loving voice, I'll go to sleep each night trusting in you.
Psalm 143:7–8 MSG

Date:

Good morning, God!

As I begin my day, I want to share. . .

I'm feeling. . .

Please infuse my heart with Your joy!

Help me to accomplish. . .

I am fully giving these worries and concerns to You...

Thank You for...

Other things I need to share with You, God...

Thank You, Father, for hearing my prayers. Amen.

Because I am righteous, I will see you. When I awake,
I will see you face to face and be satisfied.
PSALM 17:15 NLT

Date:

Good morning, God!

As I begin my day, I want to share. . .

I'm feeling. . .

Please infuse my heart with Your joy!

Help me to accomplish. . .

I am fully giving these worries and concerns to You. . .

Thank You for. . .

Other things I need to share with You, God. . .

Thank You, Father, for hearing my prayers. *Amen.*

"Awake, O sleeper, rise up from the dead, and Christ will give you light."
EPHESIANS 5:14 NLT

Date:

Good morning, God!

As I begin my day, I want to share. . .

I'm feeling. . .

Please infuse my heart with Your joy!

Help me to accomplish. . .

I am fully giving these worries and concerns to You. . .

Thank You for. . .

Other things I need to share with You, God. . .

Thank You, Father, for hearing my prayers. Amen.

I pray to God—my life a prayer—
and wait for what he'll say and do.
Psalm 130:5 MSG

Date:

Good morning, God!

As I begin my day, I want to share. . .

I'm feeling. . .

Please infuse my heart with Your joy!

Help me to accomplish. . .

I am fully giving these worries and concerns to You. . .

Thank You for. . .

Other things I need to share with You, God. . .

Thank You, Father, for hearing my prayers. *Amen.*

God remains the strength of my heart; he is mine forever.
PSALM 73:26 NLT